STARTING A CHILD CARE CENTER

The Indispensable Guidebook for Starting A Day Care or Child Care Business

by

Dr. Millicent Gray Lownes-Jackson

Edited by

Dr. Leah Grubbs

A BUSINESS OF YOUR OWN ®
BUSINESS PUBLICATIONS AND SERVICES FOR WOMEN
WWW.WOMANINBIZ.COM

COPYRIGHT © 2004

COPYRIGHT © 2004, 2003, 1998, 1986 by

A BUSINESS OF YOUR OWN ®

ALL RIGHTS ARE RESERVED. NO PART OF THIS PUBLICATION MAY BE REPRODUCED OR TRANSMITTED IN ANY FORM OR BY ANY MEANS WITHOUT THE WRITTEN PERMISSION OF THE PUBLISHER, A BUSINESS OF YOUR OWN,
P. O. BOX 210662, NASHVILLE, TN 37221-0662.
ISBN 0-943267-17-X

A Business of Your Own

OUR SYMBOL   **A ROSE OF PURPLE**

A BUSINESS OF YOUR OWN will help you till the soil and prepare fertile ground for the growth and development of a strong and successful business venture. It will take time. It will take shrewd business savvy. It will take planning and re-planning and it will take an honest assessment of yourself.

Rose gardens don't just happen overnight. A rose, purple in color, demands very special attention and a great amount of time for development and much nurturing. But, there are few flowers more special that a beautiful, unique rose. The cultivation of a beautiful purple rose is representative of the development of your successful business venture.

The purple rose is distinctive and different. It represents newness, freshness, femininity, and taking the challenge to be different.

Women have intrinsic characteristics that, like a purple rose, can be cultivated. These characteristics can be channeled into a viable avenue of financial independence. But, a woman does not have to lose her uniqueness of being a woman.

A rose of purple, just like a business, requires much time, attention, dedication, knowledge, and nurturing. **A BUSINESS OF YOUR OWN** is here to help you in developing your unique rose.

"Our goals are to help cultivate your abilities, assist you in channeling your attributes successfully into a business of your own, encourage you to be the best you can be, provide information to help make you successful in the business world and at the same time encourage you to maintain your identity and femininity."
                                                  M.G.L.J.

A Business of Your Own
BUSINESS PUBLICATIONS & SERVICES FOR WOMEN
P.O.B. 210662
Nashville, Tennessee 37221-0662
WWW.WOMANINBIZ.COM
E-mail: Success@womaninbiz.com

IT'S YOUR TIME!

It's time for you to assume your rightful seat on the throne,

leading a business of your own.

M.G.L.J.

CONGRATULATIONS!!!

By merely opening this publication you have taken the first step toward self-fulfilment, financial independence and taking control of your life. You obviously have an interest in small business ownership and desire to take the informative approach to starting your own business. Effective application of the information presented in this publication will enable you to fulfill your dream of business ownership and financial success. This publication will take you step-by-step through the process of business formulation. At the end of your reading, you will have produced a business plan for your dream and will have identified the specific steps you need to take for implementing your business to be competitive.

A BUSINESS OF YOUR OWN is here to help you pull together the intricate components necessary to make your small business a success. We offer various support services as well as numerous business publications to assist you in pursuit of your entrepreneurial dreams.

We invite you to take the entrepreneurial challenge and wish you much success!

www.WomanInBiz.com
Mailing address: P.O.B. 210662, Nashville, Tennessee, 37221-0662 (615) 646-3708

"To teach and care for a child is to

TOUCH A LIFE FOREVER."

M.G.L.J.

INFORMATION ABOUT THIS PUBLICATION

The entrepreneurial informational publications of A BUSINESS OF YOUR OWN reflect an enormous amount of in-depth research and the expertise of many noted professionals. In addition to keeping abreast of industry and environmental changes along with new business management techniques and concepts, our staff compiles and presents this information in a readily applicable, easy-to-understand format. Obtaining detailed industry information as presented in our publications would have taken your complete business venture concentration for many, many months. In addition, by purchasing our publications you will avoid the costs that would have been incurred in consulting many professionals and the stress encountered in determining business development procedures.

All information contained in this publication will need to be applied to your particular operating environment as each environment is unique and exciting. We, therefore, cannot accept responsibility for your success; but we truly believe that the information and the step-by-step approach utilized in this publication will assist you in making more intelligent decisions about the initiation and development of your business.

Even though all companies, resources, and organizations mentioned in this book are believed to be reputable, A BUSINESS OF YOUR OWN cannot accept responsibility for the activities of these parties, nor is A BUSINESS OF YOUR OWN attempting to promote their business efforts.

Congratulations on taking the first step to business success by obtaining the necessary knowledge to realize your dreams.

"Teachers should teach children to do more than just count; they should teach children what counts--INTEGRITY."

M.G.L.J.

TABLE OF CONTENTS

PAGE NUMBER

CHAPTER I	***INTRODUCTION***	*10*
	Industry Overview	14
	Parental Concerns	16
	Questions Parents Ask	18
	Equipment and Facilities	18
	Meals/Daily Routine/Training/Insurance	20
	Transportation	21
	Inspection	21
	An Ideal Child Care Center	21
	The Student Selection Process	24
	Financial Records	25
	The Accounting Process	26
	Financial Statements	27
	Businesses and Child Care	28
	Information Worth Knowing	30
CHAPTER II	***CONSIDERING THE CHALLENGE***	*32*
	Qualities Necessary for Success in Small Business	35
	Successful Leadership Traits	42
	Characteristics of Successful Small Business Managers	44
	Professional Requirements for Success in Small Business	44
	Motivation of Entrepreneurs	46
	Evaluating Yourself	48
	Selecting The Type of Business To Enter	61
	Assessing Your Monetary Requirements	68
CHAPTER III	***THE BUSINESS PLAN***	*74*
	The Business	77
	Financial Data	78
	Supporting Documents	78
	Business Plan Worksheets	79
CHAPTER IV	***MARKETING***	*92*
	Surveying the Market	96
	Sample Questionnaire	97
	Advertising Guidelines	103
	Measuring the Results of Advertising	104
	Marketing Research	106
	Examining the Economic Environment for Your Business	110
CHAPTER V	***FORMS OF BUSINESS OWNERSHIP***	*112*
	Proprietorship	114
	Partnership	115

	Corporation	117
	S Corporation	118
	Limited Liability Company	119
	Franchising	121
CHAPTER VI	***TAKING OVER AN ESTABLISHED BUSINESS***	***128***
	New Business versus An Established Business	130
	Acquiring An Established Business	130
	How To Enter An Existing Business	132
CHAPTER VII	***LOCATION***	***136***
	Reaching Potential Customers	138
	Location Considerations	140
CHAPTER VIII	***STAFFING***	***142***
	Application for Employment	146
	Employee Relations	148
	Employee Handbook	149
	Resume for Principals	151
CHAPTER IX	***ORGANIZING YOUR BUSINESS***	***154***
	Ways of Organizing Your Business	157
CHAPTER X	***FINANCING YOUR BUSINESS***	***160***
	Pointers for Successful Debt Financing	170
CHAPTER XI	***BUSINESS RECORDS***	***172***
	Income Statement	176
	Capital Statement	177
	Balance Sheet	178
CHAPTER XII	***SOURCES OF SUPPLY AND INVENTORY***	***182***
CHAPTER XIII	***SALES FORECASTING***	***186***
CHAPTER XIV	***THE INVESTMENT PROSPECTUS***	***190***
CHAPTER XV	***IS IT FEASIBLE?***	***194***
CHAPTER XVI	***CONCLUSION***	***200***
CHAPTER XVII	***BUSINESS GLOSSARY***	***210***
CHAPTER XVIII	***BUSINESS RESOURCES***	***222***
APPENDIX	***SAMPLE BUSINESS FORMS***	***242***

CHAPTER I

Introduction

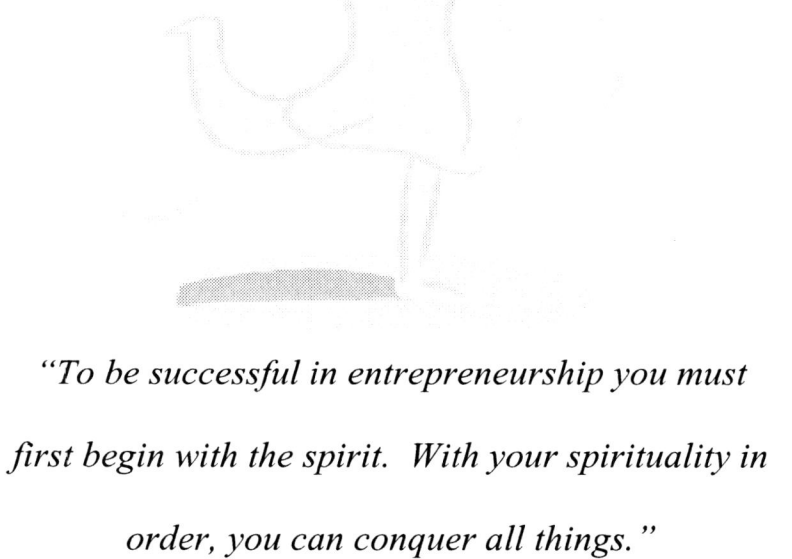

"To be successful in entrepreneurship you must first begin with the spirit. With your spirituality in order, you can conquer all things."

M.G.L.J.

INTRODUCTION

The quest for business ownership is still very much a part of the American dream, and the entrepreneurial spirit is alive and strong for women. Offering for many, a feeling of personal worth, wealth, prestige, and a way of controlling one's own time and destiny, female-owned businesses represent the fastest growing business sector of the economy. Recent private research conducted by the Center for Women's Business Research reports that, as of 2002, there were an estimated 10.1 million majority-owned, privately held 50 percent or more women-owned firms in the United States, employing 18.2 million people and generating $2.32 trillion in sales. Of this 10.1 million, 6.2 million are majority (51%) or more women-owned, and 3.9 million are 50 percent women-owned firms. As of 2002, there were an estimated 1.2 million firms owned by a woman or women of color-amounting to 1 in 5 women-owned firms (20%) in the U.S. Overall, the number of minority women-owned firms increased by 32 percent between 1997 and 2002-four times faster than all U.S. firms and over twice the rate of all women-owned firms. Between 1997 and 2002, the Center estimates that the number of privately held 50 percent or more women-owned firms increased by 11 percent nationwide, nearly twice the rate of all firms, employment increased by 18 percent, and sales grew by 32 percent. [1]

Census Department data uses different definitions for women-owned businesses, requiring that the business be 51 percent owned by a woman before it is classified as woman owned. Thus, Census data reports a fewer number of women-owned businesses, but the bottom line is that women-owned businesses are playing a vital role in the U.S. economy. Women-owned businesses are growing more rapidly than the overall economy and are major contributors to the nation's economic health and competitiveness. Many of these women-owned firms are considered to be micro-enterprises, small businesses with fewer than five employees. Generally, these businesses are characterized by a net worth of less than $25,000 and a credit need of less than $15,000. Many of the business owners are women who are underemployed or have low incomes.

National research recently conducted by this writer utilizing survey research methodology provides additional insight into practical entrepreneurial knowledge. Surveys were disseminated via a national business publication as well as a local community newspaper. The survey was designed to ascertain pressing concerns, problems and stressors experienced by female business owners. A summarization of the findings indicates the following areas of concern as identified by female micro-enterprise owners: organizational ability, selling skills, finding and keeping good employees, managing stress, inequities due to race or sex, inability to obtain government and corporate accounts, inability to break the "ole boy" network, inability to obtain sufficient capital, inability to effectively and efficiently manage operating expenses, feeling isolated, managing time, and the challenge of accepting all responsibility. The issues and concerns raised by this survey population of 200 female micro-enterprise owners reflect the views of those who have taken the entrepreneurial plunge and have provided a sound academic and practical base for compiling the relevant and valuable information contained in this publication.

INDUSTRY OVERVIEW

The intricate fibers making up the child care tapestry in America are vibrant and varied, consisting of many different early-learning and child care options for parents. Some of the common types of child care alternatives available to parents include nonprofit and profit centers, faith-based and faith-sponsored centers, corporate-sponsored centers, family child care homes, nursery schools, nannies, care by family members, and government-sponsored child care programs. Additionally, the nature of child care ranges from infant and toddler care, to pre-school, kindergarten, 24-hour care, and after school care. There are also centers that focus on a specific type of care, such as care for special needs children or care for seriously ill children or simply temporary special care for children with minor illnesses, such as the flu or a simple bad cold, who cannot attend their normal child care due to center policies regarding attendance when sick.

The need for child care continues to grow. According to the most recent statistics available from U.S. Census Bureau, as of November 2000 there were 18,945,000 children under the age of 5 years in the United States.[2] The Census Bureau also reports that approximately 30 percent of the nation's children receive care in organized child care facilities such as child care centers and nursery schools.

Varied national data sources indicate that more than half of all women with children under the age of six have jobs outside the home. In other words, most American mothers are not at home with their children. Women are in the labor force to stay and resultantly, the need for quality, affordable child care continues to increase. According to the Children's Foundation 2003 Child Care Center Licensing Study, there are 116,409 regulated child care centers in the 50 States, District of Columbia, Puerto Rico, and Virgin Islands. The 2003 Study shows a 26 percent increase from 1991 in the number of regulated centers nationwide.[3]

For the purpose of clarification, the following definitions are presented and will be used throughout this publication.

Child Care - The term child care can refer to a wide variety of arrangements made by parents or guardians for the care of children outside of the home for less than 24 hours. Child care services may be offered by family or group child care homes, child care or child development centers, nursery schools, day nurseries, kindergartens, and agencies providing before- and after-school are. The terms day care and child care are quite often used interchangeably.

Child - A person under 17 years of age.

Preschool Child - A person five years of age or younger.

Infant - A child who is less than 15 months old and not walking.

Toddler - A child who is between 15 and 35 months of age and walking.

School Age Child - A person who is at least five years of age and in kindergarten to grade six.

Primary Caregiver - Any person who is in charge of operating the child care facility.

Family Child Care Home - A home operated by any person who receives five or more children who are not related to the person and whose parents or guardians are not residents of the same house. The person has the children for less than 24 hours a day for care without transfer of custody.

Group Child Care Home - Any place operated by a person, social agency, corporation, institution, or other group which receives eight or more children for less than 24 hours per day for care without transfer of custody.

Child Care Center - A facility operated by a person, agency, corporation or any other group that receives pay for the care of 13 or more children for less than 24 hours a day without transfer of custody.

Drop-In Centers - Facilities that provide casual care for no more than 15 children, not to exceed 10 hours per week and not for more than 6 hours per day for any individual child while parents or other custodians are engaged in short-term activities. Drop-In Centers are often operated in connection with a business establishment, church, nonprofit organization, recreational facility, or similar facility.

Licensing - The rules and regulations pertaining to child care licensing vary by state. States generally require that anyone providing child care for more than a certain number of children be licensed to insure that children receive care that meets the minimum standards related to health, safety and supervision. These standards, of course, are designed for the welfare of children, but the licensed, quality child care program does reap many advantages, including obtaining a good reputation and the chance to obtain referrals from the State Department providing licensure.

In designing your child care program, you must not only adhere to your state child care program requirements, but you should also take into consideration the following concerns generally expressed by parents about child care facilities.

PARENTAL CONCERNS

The categorized listings which follow include areas of parental concerns which must be addressed.

THE CHILD CARE PROGRAM

- Learning activities, materials and equipment (the total nature of the educational program).
- Learning format (Do children work in groups or alone?).

- Play format (group play, individual play time and types of play activities).
- Number and caliber of staff (educational background, training and number of personnel).
- Compatibility of program values with family values.
- Opening and closing times.
- The role parents can take with the program.
- Transportation provisions
- The daily routine.

SAFETY, HEALTH, NUTRITION

- Is the firm licensed?
- The physical facility, including its cleanliness, neatness, appropriateness for learning and amount of space.
- Safety of equipment, materials and the facility in general.
- Nutrition and nature of meals.
- Snacks.
- Nap time and rest area.
- Play area.

INTERPERSONAL INTERACTIONS

- Compatibility of provider's personality with child.
- Child-rearing philosophy of the care provider.
- Manner in which discipline is handled.
- How children are treated in general in terms of caring, encouragement, attention, etc.

THE FEE

- What is included in the fee? Does it cover lunch, field trips, etc.?
- Is the fee competitive with other care providers?

Additionally, parents of certain age groups will have different types of concerns based on the needs of the age group. Parents of infants will be particularly concerned about feeding, diapering, individual attention, educational toys, and interaction with other children. Parents of preschool children will be more concerned with the learning process, encouragement of creativity and meaningful interaction with other children. Parents of school-age children will be interested in learning activities, the overseeing of homework completion, skill improvement programming, tutoring programs, cultural programs, such as foreign languages, sports and play activities.

QUESTIONS PARENTS FREQUENTLY ASK

- Is the center licensed?
- If the center is licensed, is the license in good standing?
- What experience and training do the care givers have?
- How long has the center been in operation?
- What recreational and educational activities are included in the program?
- What discipline approach does the center take?
- What type and amount of food does the center serve?
- How many children is each care giver responsible for?
- Are there parents to call for references?
- Has the center ever lost its license or received violation citations?

EQUIPMENT AND FACILITIES

Your state Department of Human Services and/or state and local governing child care agencies can provide you with specific equipment and facility requirements. All equipment and furniture must be well made and safe. All equipment should be age appropriate, must be kept clean and in good repair with no sharp edges, splinters or nails sticking out. Damaged equipment should be removed and repaired immediately. The following equipment list is presented as a guide to basic equipment needs. Realize that your equipment as well as your facility needs will vary based on age groups and environmental requirements. Most states provide specific guidelines for general equipment as well as play equipment.

FURNITURE

Child-sized tables and chairs.

Shelves.

Cots and foam mats.

Shelves for toys.

Cribs.

Play pens.

High chairs.

TOYS

Toys for quiet play.	Tools for cooking.
Toys for active play.	Tools for yard work.
Toys for make believe.	Supplies for sewing and handicrafts.
Learning materials.	Art supplies.
Books.	Music.
Basic school supplies.	

MEALS

Many child care providers have found food service laws, standards and health codes so stringent that contracting with outside firms for this service has become more and more popular. This is an option you may want to consider as well.

DAILY ROUTINE

Studies have shown that all children should have a consistent daily schedule as it provides security for them and tends to reduce behavioral problems. This does not mean that the routine cannot be changed occasionally. The daily routine for toddlers and preschoolers should consist of teacher-directed activities for the whole group, indoor and out-door play time, active and quiet play, play time in interest centers, teacher-directed activities and child-chosen activities, snacks, meals, and rest time.

TRAINING

Most state Departments of Human Services and/or state child care agencies offer courses, conferences, seminars, and publications to assist child care providers in keeping up to date on current information.

INSURANCE

Professional liability and accident insurance are increasingly expensive and are sometimes difficult to obtain. The possibility of your obtaining insurance coverage increases as your program exceeds the licensing requirements of your state. Surpassing standard requirements helps convince insurance companies that your operation is not a bad risk. Insurance liability issues are even greater if you elect to provide transportation.

TRANSPORTATION

If you decide to offer transportation services, you need to be cognizant of the intensity of the responsibility associated with such services. In addition to the tremendous general responsibility of transporting children and liability issues, most states have laws and specific requirements that must be adhered to which may include the number of adults that must be present during transport, restraint devices, special licenses and special endorsements, just to mention a few concern areas.

INSPECTIONS

Licensed child care agencies are inspected in many states a minimum of six times a year with unannounced visits to ensure that they continue to meet licensing requirements. Agencies are also investigated in response to complaints. Child care agencies are required to post their license, and the child care report card issued by many states, in a conspicuous place where parents can see them.

AN IDEAL CHILD CARE CENTER
(FOR SOME STATES)

The following standards are provided to offer a general sense of requirements of some states. You should contact your state regulatory agency for specifics for your state, city, or town and service group.

Infants (10 children)

- Two rooms, each 14 feet by 14 feet.

- Two age groups: 6 weeks to 6 months and 6 months to 12 months.

- Five beds in each room.

- Changing area with cubbies, a sink in each room and storage and refrigeration central to both rooms.

- Toy storage in both rooms.

- Breastfeeding area in each room. (Many mothers desire to interact with their infants during the day and breastfeed their babies.)

- Two teachers and one aide who floats between the two rooms.

Toddlers (14 children)

- Two rooms, each 17 feet by 17 feet.

- Two age groups: 12 months to 18 months (seven children) and 18 months to 24 months (seven children).

- Changing area with cubbies in both rooms.

- Toilet training area.

- Bathroom central to both rooms with two to three toilets.

- Storage area central to both rooms.

- Sink in each room.

- Low windows and low storage bins.

- Two teachers and one aide who floats between the two rooms.

Two-Year Olds (16 children)

- Two rooms, each 17 feet by 17 feet.

- Two groups of eight children.
- Low sink and cubbies in each room.
- Storage area.
- Two-stall bathroom.
- Tables and chairs (child-sized).
- Two teachers and one aide who floats between two rooms.

Threes and Fours (15 children) - one room

Fours and Fives (15 children) - one room

- Three, four and five-year olds can utilize partitioned rooms, each approximately 31 feet by 17 feet.
- Shared bathrooms and shared interest areas in each room.
- Two teachers and one aide who floats between the two rooms.
- All rooms need wide exits to the outside with crash doors. Corridors need to meet fire code regulations. Additional requirements include kitchen, director's office, reception area, and teacher's lounge/restroom.

Sick Care

- Approximately five cribs and 15 beds.
- Approximately 900 square feet of segregated space in four wards of approximately 225 feet each
- A common area.
- Nursing station.

- Ample bathrooms and sink areas in segregated spaces.
- One registered nurse (preferred) or LPN with adequate experience.
- Two assistants (preferably one with medical and one with child care training).

THE STUDENT SELECTION PROCESS

The number and ages of the children you care for will relate to your desires, abilities, facilities, personnel resources, and regulations for your area. All children will need to have on file an application form, health form, a signed contract and other necessary forms based on state and local requirements and the requirements you establish for your center. Sample forms are included in the appendix for your convenience.

FINANCES

Of course, adequate financing must be maintained for the center's operation. Many states require that centers make available an annual operating budget including a statement of income and expenditures. Many child care programs depend on outside funding for partial or total support. Owners of child care businesses need to have skill in proposal writing to offset costs not covered by tuitions. Many child care programs receive monies via grants from foundations or the government, United Way funds, community organizations and charities, as well as sponsoring agencies. Contact your local United Way agency to obtain eligibility requirements and application forms to apply for funding. To get a handle on other funding sources, talk with directors of operating child care centers to determine their funding base, consult the Directory of Grants and Foundations and your local public library, and talk with officials in your state Department of Human Services.

FINANCIAL RECORDS

The need for child care services and child care businesses is evident, but the need and demand for such services is not necessarily sufficient for the success of a child care business. Of course, satisfying a need is an important ingredient and a starting point for evaluating the feasibility of a venture. Attention must be directed toward the internal management of the child care business. Businesses fail for many reasons, but poor management, which includes financial management, is one of the major contributing factors to failure. Thus, the crucial nature of effectively managing the financial aspect of the child care business is obvious.

Financial records tell the child care business owner/manager what the business is doing financially at all times and will direct the manager's attention to problem areas. A good manager needs to know what these records reflect so that problems can be detected and remedies implemented before the business experiences financial destruction.

In spite of the obvious importance of developing accounting records, many small firms do not maintain them adequately. It has been discovered, for example, that small firms which have gone bankrupt typically had inadequate accounting records. On the other hand, small firms which maintain adequate records, generally reflect high-quality management because such records provide management a basis for more effective decision making and better control over operating results.

Objectives of an Accounting System

An accounting system should accomplish the following objectives:

1. It should yield an accurate, thorough picture of operating results.

2. The records should permit comparisons of the current year's performance with prior years and with budgetary goals.

3. The records should provide financial statements for use by management, bankers, and creditors.

4. The system should reveal employee fraud, thefts, waste, and record keeping errors.

The Accounting Process

In order to provide useful information about a business enterprise, we need some means of keeping track of the daily business activities and then summarizing the results in accounting reports. The methods used by a business to keep records of its financial activities and to summarize these activities in periodic accounting reports comprise the accounting system.

The first function of an accounting system is to create a systematic record of the daily business activity, in terms of money. For example, goods and services are purchased and sold, credit is extended to customers, debts are incurred, and cash is received and paid out. These transactions are typical business events which can be expressed in monetary terms and must be entered in accounting records. In addition to compiling a narrative record of events as they occur, we classify transactions and events in related groups or categories called accounts. Classification enables us to reduce a mass of detail into compact and usable form. For example, grouping all transactions in which cash is received or paid out is a logical step in developing useful information about the cash position of a business enterprise. To organize accounting information in a useful form, we summarize the classified information into accounting reports designed to meet the information needs of decision makers. These three steps we have described -- recording, classifying, and summarizing--are the means of creating accounting information. More details on this follow in the business record section of this publication.

Financial Statements

The two principal reports resulting from the process of accounting are the balance sheet and the income statement. The **balance sheet** is designed to portray the financial position of the firm at a particular point in time. It lists the **assets** or **resources** owned by the company, the **debts** of the firm and **owner's interest (equity)** in the company (i.e. the resources invested in the business by the owner).

The **income statement** shows the amount of income earned by a business over a period of time. Many people consider it the most important financial report because its purpose is to measure whether or not the business achieved or failed its primary objective of earning an acceptable income. The statement is divided into two basic sections: **revenues** and **expenses**. **Revenue** represents the total amount obtained from the goods sold and services rendered to customers. In the case of a child care center, the major source of revenues is in the form of tuition and fees charged for child care services rendered. The center may not only receive funds from parents, but may also receive funding from governmental agencies such as welfare agencies. **Expenses** are the cost of the goods and services used up in the process of obtaining revenue. **Net income** is the difference between total revenues and total expenses. If revenues are greater, the company will report net income. If expenses are greater, the company will report a net loss for the period.

It is recommended that the services of a qualified bookkeeper and an accountant be obtained to ensure proper accounting system development and maintenance. You will also need to decide if you want your records kept manually, computerized or a combination of both.

BUSINESSES AND CHILD CARE

Day care has perhaps become one of the more popular benefits offered to employees by corporate America. Businesses have come to the realization that if their employees have to be concerned about their children's whereabouts after school and/or their care during the day, a productivity drain results--a drain in terms of time, attention and energy. Many potentially good workers even decide not to work when the cost of child care and related expenses are evaluated. In essence, child care problems negatively affect the worker leading to a negative effect on a business's bottom line or profit. Many large corporations and small businesses, as well, have determined that assisting employees with child care is cost-effective.

The types of child care assistance offered by companies can take on many forms. Some of the child care assistance benefits offer wonderful promotional opportunities for the creative entrepreneur. The more common types of child care offered to employees include the following:

Informational Assistance

Many firms offer child care referral services to assist workers in locating child care. Additionally, some businesses offer educational seminars and counseling to help employees manage their responsibilities to their family and to their job.

Financial Assistance

A great number of businesses reduce the costs of child care by making direct or indirect contributions.

Flexible Personnel Policies

Some firms help with the child care dilemma by offering flexible scheduling such as job sharing, flex-time and compressed work weeks, permanent part-time positions, family leave policies, paternity and maternity leave. These policies are designed to help reduce the employee's need for child care services.

Direct Child Care Services

Many businesses have moved to the point of actually offering child care services at the work site. This is the most common form of direct child care. Some businesses also operate child care programs in homes and in schools for employees, as well as programs for sick children and summer camps for school-age children.

Salary Reduction

Some firms are allowing employees to assign part of their salary to a salary-reduction account which allows the employee to pay for child care with their pre-tax dollars.

Combination Programs

Of course, many combinations of these programs can be found in the benefits package of employees.

The reasons why businesses have made child care their concern are many and varied; however, they can basically be summarized as follows:

-- Improved staff morale.
-- Lower employee turnover.
-- Lower absenteeism and tardiness.
-- Good public relations for the company.
-- Good recruitment tool.
-- Greater productivity.

INFORMATION WORTH KNOWING

- There is a growing trend of 24-hour child care programs along with programs for sick children.

- In cities and towns where there are a great number of people working shifts, shift child care is growing in popularity.

- Contact your state Department of Agriculture for information about their food supplement programs for lower and middle income students.

- Contact your state Department of Human Services (DHS) for information about grant money to help subsidize fees required for lower and middle income students.

- Satellite child care programs for infants are a growing trend. These programs operate under the auspices of a child care organization, but homes are used to take care of infants.

- Day care for ages 6 weeks to two and a half represents a great child care need area.

- It's less expensive to care for three-, four- and five-year olds because the student-teacher ratio and space requirements tend to be lower in many states.

- More successful child care programs are designed so that children can "feed up." In essence, children can start in the program at the infant stage and continue with the program up until school age. This cuts down on the need for marketing to attract students in the older age groups.

- Most parents prefer educationally formed programs.

- Prior to approaching an insurance company for coverage, make sure you can show them a good business plan that includes a procedural program for screening, orienting and training employees. This helps in proving to the insurance company that its risk is minimized.

- Investigate contracting with a firm for meal service.

- The rules and standards governing child care become more intense when you rise above a prescribed number of children. Examine the requirements in your area for the different levels and organize your center based on what is feasible for you.

The world of child care is exciting with many self-fulfilling dimensions along with business challenges. Let's get prepared for the challenges.

"There is no fast, challenge-free, road to success. You have to take it one step at a time and overcome one challenge at a time and turn the challenges into opportunities to determine your inner strength."

M.G.L.J.

CHAPTER II

Considering the Challenge

THE ENTREPRENEURIAL CHALLENGE

*Business ownership is **a challenging, exhilarating, yet exhausting** way of life. The road to business success is filled with **risk, problems and pitfalls**. The business owner **must meet these frustrations with perseverance**. An attitude of perseverance, in light of future rewards, helps the business owner to continue the commitment to business. **Perseverance, continual planning and hard work** enable the business owner to overcome the obstacles inherent in any new venture.*

***Small business ownership can be a reality for you**. Identify your passion, turn your passion into a profitable venture through planning and, above all, persevere to create **a business of your own that fulfills your dreams** for the future.*

ON TO THE CHALLENGE....

CONSIDERING THE CHALLENGE

"Like creating the intricate components of a computer system or cultivating a rose garden, pulling together all the elements of a successful small business is an art that requires knowledge, skill, hard work, experience and much determination." MGLJ

Are you an individualist, an independent-type of person, an adventurer? Are you a risk taker? Do you dislike taking common orders and doing the same thing every day? Do you like the freedom of working independently? Do you like testing your own talents and reaping benefits directly from your personal efforts? Do you desire to use your ideas, abilities, ambitions, aspirations, and initiative to the greatest degree? If you answer "yes" to most of these questions, then maybe you need to consider owning "a business of your own."

Are you are tired of your present work environment or tired of the routine? Do you feel that you are in a rut? Do you feel that your abilities go overlooked? Maybe you simply desire a chance to make more money. Perhaps you think you have a good idea for a business. Are you a displaced homemaker needing to find a way to support yourself? Or do you just have spare time on your hands? If any of these examples fits you, then small business ownership may be the answer allowing you to realize many of your dreams.

There is no question that all people are not qualified to be business owners, nor is there any question that persons who wish to establish a business must depend on their own qualifications and abilities to "make it" or "break it." Going into business is a major decision requiring much commitment.

Business-success potential is highly related to the personal attributes of the business owner. Many studies have been conducted regarding the personal requirements necessary for small business success. Certain common characteristics have been found among successful women who have started businesses. Successful entrepreneurs tend to be decisive and versatile. They follow tasks through to completion. They are self-confident. They are persistent. They have knowledge of the fields in which they start their businesses. They have a strong degree of drive. They are creative and analytical thinkers and have good human relations skills.

AM I DESCRIBING YOU?

Women must realize that they have many inherent talents and abilities which are often taken for granted and have exceptional transferability to the business world. Women have unique talents and skills, instilled during childhood, which may be reflected in their daily life styles and which may be channeled effectively into a business venture. Simple activities normally taken for granted, such as managing the home and managing children, coordinating activities for social organizations, the ability to do ten things at one time, delegating chores and responsibilities at work or at home, organizing a car pool, keeping the boss organized, or being responsible, reliable, and economical are all abilities that frequently go unappreciated and overlooked. They are sometimes even looked down on because they are viewed as being traditional female values or female stereotyping. But, ladies, whether you view yourself as liberated or not, we need to look at ourselves and assess all of these abilities which can easily be transferred into dollars in the business world.

All of us have unique abilities and skills. An in-depth, self-evaluation process will allow you to identify your strongest areas and focus on interests and abilities which could be channeled strategically and successfully into a business venture. This process is a necessity prior to starting a business.

Later in this chapter we will proceed with this process and examine your qualities in light of the characteristics common among successful entrepreneurs. But let's first review the research related to entrepreneurial success characteristics.

Individuals contemplating going into business for themselves should be aware of the personal attributes required for success as an entrepreneur. Numerous studies suggest that there are certain personal requirements or personality characteristics which successful small business owner-managers seem to have in common. One such study was conducted by a team of psychologists at Case Western Reserve University. This study utilized tests, questionnaires, and in-depth interviews and examined characteristics of chief executive officers of several successful small businesses. The study resulted in the following profile of the successful entrepreneur:[4]

1. The successful entrepreneur is a moderate risk taker-- not a gambler. He{or she} is an adventurer.

2. The successful small business person is decisive and tends to like tight control over decision making.

3. The successful small business person is versatile and tends to strive for competence in many business areas.

4. The successful small business person is a finisher. He{or she} tends to have strong motives to achieve and endure until the completion of a task.

5. The successful small business person is self-confident. He {or she} has a strong belief in his own capabilities.

6. The successful business person is a benevolent despot, and he{or she} tends to be friendly willing to listen to the suggestions of subordinates.

Another study of personality characteristics that lead to success in small business was made by H. B. Pickle. He identifies five characteristics he considers significant.[5]

1. Drive--comprised of responsibility, vigor, initiative, persistence and health;

2. Thinking Ability--comprised of original or creative analytical thinking;

3. Human Relations Ability--comprised of ascendancy, emotional stability, sociability, cautiousness, consideration, cheerfulness, cooperation and tact;

4. Communications Ability--both oral and written; and

5. Technical Knowledge--comprised of acquired skills developed through study and practical application.

A review of the literature on small business initiation, ownership and management leads to the conclusion that there are various personal attributes necessary for success in entrepreneurship. The Small Business Administration (SBA), the governmental agency which assists small businesses, identifies certain personal attributes as being necessary for entrepreneurial success. Included in the list are the following 18 characteristics and abilities:

1. Ability and understanding of others,

2. Willingness to take a chance,

3. Ability to withstand stress,

4. Ability to take over when the going gets rough,
5. Honesty in business relationships,
6. Selling skills,
7. Spirit to meet competition,
8. Ability to keep abreast of new technology in the field, as well as environmental changes,
9. Initiative and leadership abilities,
10. High capability for organizing,
11. Industriousness and capability to work long hours,
12. Ability to make and guide accurate decisions,
13. Perseverance (not discouraged by obstacles),
14. Desire to get ahead with a high level of energy,
15. Ability to understand customers and their desires,
16. Ability to adapt to change,
17. Innovativeness, and
18. Ability to inspire and direct or motivate[6]

There has been considerable interest in the nature of the entrepreneur for many years, but interest in the female entrepreneur has surfaced only recently. This interest has been generated by the recognition that the entrepreneur is a central figure in economic activity. However, relatively little research has been done on the female entrepreneur, and much of the research conducted has been based on perceptual responses rather than objective measurements.

Hornaday and Aboud made attempts to develop and identify objective tests which were valid and which would not require administration by a psychologist. They found that the achievement scale of the Edwards Personal Preference Schedule and the Support, Independence and Leadership scales of the Gordon Survey of Interpersonal Values held promise for distinguishing between entrepreneurs.[7]

Decarlo and Lyons conducted research using Hornaday and Aboud's research as a guide. They compared selected personal characteristics of minority and non-minority female entrepreneurs. The characteristics on which noticeable differences occurred were:[8]

1. Age of entrepreneur--The minority females were somewhat older than their non-minority counterparts.

2. Age at the time of starting a business--The minority females reported they started their businesses at a later age than non-minority females.

3. Previous entrepreneurial effort--Almost twice as many minority females as non-minority females reported that their current businesses were not their first entrepreneurial effort.

4. Marriage rate--A greater proportion of the non-minority females reported never having been married. This is contrary to the 1975 Census data that reported half again as many black women as white women had never been married.

5. Educational experience--A greater proportion of non-minority females reported having graduated from both high school and college. Both groups reported a higher education level than the Census had reported for all females in 1975. According to the Census, only 64 percent of all females over age 25 had completed four years of high school or more. The minority females, however, reported being more active than non-minority females in extracurricular activities and were responsible for personally financing their college educations.

6. Acceptance regimentation--A much greater percentage of minority females reported a willingness to accept regimentation than did the non-minority females. This may reflect the fact that female entrepreneurs represent a distinct minority in the business world.

7. Means of starting a business--The minority women were much more likely than the non-minority women to have started their businesses alone than with a partner.

When non-minority female entrepreneurs were compared to minority female entrepreneurs on the nine scales of achievement, autonomy, aggression, support, conformity, recognition, independence, benevolence, and leadership, it was found that significant differences existed on six of the nine scales. The non-minority females placed a higher value on the scales of achievement, support, recognition, and independence, whereas the minority females placed a higher value on the conformity and benevolence scales.[9]

John Mancuso has studied a group of 300 entrepreneurs for several years. He has concluded that the typical successful entrepreneur can be described as follows:[10]

1. The entrepreneur is the first-born child in his or her family.
2. The entrepreneur is married, with a supportive spouse.
3. The entrepreneur began his or her first company at the age of 30 or so.
4. Entrepreneurial tendencies manifested themselves during the teenage years.
5. The level of education varies among entrepreneurs. The technical entrepreneur often has a master's degree. The typical entrepreneur probably has at least a high school and probably a college degree.
6. The entrepreneur's primary motivation for going into business for herself or himself is a psychological inability to work for anyone else.
7. The entrepreneur's personality developed mainly in interaction with his or her father's personality.

8. The successful entrepreneur is often lucky.

9. The entrepreneur seeks advice, if it is needed, from other entrepreneurs, consultants and college professors.

10. Entrepreneurs and money providers are often in conflict.

11. The entrepreneur is essentially a doer, not a planner.

12. The entrepreneur assumes moderate risks, not large or small ones.

Until recently, the world of the entrepreneur was almost entirely male. This remains true, but women are entering this world more frequently than in the past, now that the opportunities are more readily available and societal values have shifted so that it is acceptable for women to want to run their own businesses. James Schreier recently studied Milwaukee female entrepreneurs who created enterprises in "non-female" businesses (that is, he ignored Mary's beauty shop). He judged them by the characteristics just cited (Mancuso's study) and found the following differences.[11]

1. A stronger tendency toward self-employment in the family: 70 percent of male entrepreneurs came from a family headed by an entrepreneur; 93 percent of Schreier's female entrepreneurs did.

2. Seventy-two percent of the female entrepreneurs liked school, whereas the male entrepreneurs (non-technical) did not like it.

3. Male entrepreneurs become entrepreneurs because they cannot work for others, as evidenced by prior job history; 50 percent of the female entrepreneurs liked working for others in previous jobs.

4. More female entrepreneurs than male ones are divorced or single.

5. Entrepreneurial behavior manifested itself later in women but mainly because of lack of opportunity. For example, some city newspapers would not hire female paper carriers.

Entrepreneurs are, of course, leaders in their own businesses, so it is significant to examine theories pertaining to successful leadership. The following section explores two leadership trait surveys. The original survey conducted in 1948 by Stogdill, a well-known authority on leadership, reviews 24 trait studies of leadership characteristics.[12]

Successful Leadership Traits

Identified traits for successful leadership include the following:

Personality, Intelligence and Ability

In reviewing the 1948 and 1970 lists of personality characteristics, it is noted that characteristics with uniformly positive findings, which appear only in the 1948 list, are adaptability and strength of conviction. Those that appear only in the 1970 list are adjustment, aggressiveness, independence, objectivity, resourcefulness, and tolerance of stress. Characteristics that appear with positive findings in both 1948 and 1970 lists are alertness, originality, personal integrity, and self-confidence. The research consistently reports that leaders are characterized by superior judgement, decisiveness, knowledge, and fluency of speech.

Task-Oriented Characteristics

Both surveys indicate that leaders are characterized by a high need for achievement and responsibility. They tend to be very task-oriented, dependable, persistent, have initiative, drive, and are very enterprising.

Physical Characteristics

Results of recent research suggest that leaders tend to be endowed with an abundant reserve of energy, stamina and the ability to maintain a high rate of physical activity.

Social Characteristics

Leaders tend to be quite active in various social activities and get along well with others. Personality traits have been found to differentiate leaders from followers, successful from unsuccessful leaders and high-level from lower-level leaders. When considered singly, the characteristics hold very little predictive or diagnostic possibilities. But in combination, they can generate personality dynamics advantageous to the person seeking responsibilities of leadership. Examining personality as this author has, does not imply advocating a return to the trait approach to leadership in which personality variables were treated in somewhat of an isolated fashion suggesting that each trait acted independently to determine leadership effects. The author has modified the situation approach, with traits considered in conjunction with the situation.

When Stogdill analyzed 124 studies on leadership, he found that patterns of leadership traits differ, depending on the situation. According to Stogdill, "If there are general traits which characterize leaders, the patterns of such traits are likely to vary with the leadership requirements of different situations."[13]

The various research results previously cited can generally be summarized into two categories: **characteristics** and **personal requirements** for success in small business management.

Characteristics of Successful Small Business Managers

1. A great sense of independence and a desire to be independent of outside control,

2. A strong sense of enterprise which lends itself to a desire to use their ideas, abilities, ambitions, aspirations and initiatives to the greatest degree,

3. Taking their families into consideration,

4. Entrance into small business by chance rather than design,

5. Guarding their time,

6. A limited formal education, and

7. An expectation for quick results.

Professional Requirements for Success in Small Business

1. Sensitivity to internal and external changes,

2. Ability to react quickly to those changes,

3. Ability to obtain accurate and useful operating and marketing information,

4. Effective use of human resources,

5. Obtaining sufficient investment capital,

6. Effective compliance with laws,

7. Thorough understanding of the peculiarities of size,

8. Gathering industry information and keeping informed, and

9. Handling "red tape" effectively.

Motivation of Entrepreneurs

One can also look at entrepreneurs in terms of motivation theories. According to Maslow's hierarchy of needs theory, individuals move from one level to the next only after lower needs have been satisfied or nearly satisfied. Accordingly, after considerable satisfaction of basic physiological needs (hunger, thirst, etc.), the typical person would next pursue safety, social, self-esteem and finally, self-actualization needs. Research conducted by Swayne and Tucker indicates that entrepreneurs differ from the normal population. According to them, entrepreneurs seem to be strongly motivated by self-esteem and have a fairly low requirement for love, social, physiological and safety needs.[14] Going hand in hand with Maslow's theory and their findings regarding entrepreneurs, the true entrepreneur will continue to start up new ventures, and new businesses and accept new challenges even though he {or she} is financially well-off. He {or she} continues to strive for self-actualization through new and exciting ventures, and even though the finer things in life are enjoyed, the thrust is toward continuing entrepreneurial endeavors.[15]

David McClelland has devoted great efforts to examine a person's need for achievement. He {or she} has developed a need for achievement (nAch) index which can be an excellent indicator of entrepreneurial potential. Also related to nAch and entrepreneurship is the need for power (nPow) and the need for affiliation (nAff).[16]

Successful entrepreneurs also have a strong belief in their abilities to control their own lives. They do not feel that other people or conditions in the external environment can keep them from doing what they want. Julian Rotter has pioneered the development of measures for an internal-external (I-E) scale. His method involved forced choices between pairs of statements presented to a subject for evaluation. Possible scores range from 0 (extremely internal) to 23 (extremely external). Studies indicate that entrepreneurs score lower than 7 while the general population scores higher on the I-E rating. The conclusion appears to be that believing in one's ability to be successful is very important in determining entrepreneurial potential.[17]

More women than ever before are considering entrepreneurship as a career option; however, the majority of the women in the work force still think in terms of being the employee rather than the employer. Realizing that all women will not make good entrepreneurs, if you think you have the ability, a good business idea or just the desire and determination to utilize your abilities to the fullest extent, you may want to consider entrepreneurship as a career option. Entrepreneurship is indeed risky and complicated and requires much dedication. I would be remiss if I did not say that women also face many obstacles that can make the entrepreneurial road even more difficult than working a 9-5 job or staying home. Women frequently encounter credit procurement obstacles, financial barricades, and negative attitudes from male counterparts; often lack business experience; and suffer from a lack of role models and a peer support base, just to mention a few.

Even if you know you have a great business idea but realize that you may not have the personal qualities to make the idea become a reality by way of a business venture, do not abandon the thought of ownership yet. There are many entrepreneurial success qualities that can be learned and developed. To achieve business success, other qualities can be obtained by joining with other individuals who have the skills, abilities, expertise or characteristics that you may be lacking. Remember a business idea can only become a successful business with careful planning and the implementation of appropriate business knowledge, coupled with the personal characteristics necessary for small business success.

Let's now assess your skills, abilities, talents and strengths. We all have many attributes which could be very beneficial in the world of entrepreneurship, but many of these positive traits often go overlooked and unidentified. Take time to identify all of your strengths. Your strong points could include special talents, knowledge, past experience, tenacity, determination, levelheadedness, logical thinking, standing up well under stress, good communication skills, creativity, artistry, etc.

LIST YOUR STRENGTHS

(Don't be modest)

Just as you may have many personality characteristics that could help you succeed as a business owner, you may also have weaknesses which could eventually lead to entrepreneurial demise. Some of these weaknesses might include a tendency not to complete tasks you start, being more comfortable as a follower and disliking leadership responsibilities, being gullible, or too kindhearted, hating to hurt someone else's feelings even though you suffer the negative consequences, being unorganized, hating details, etc. Remember, some tendencies or traits may not have been considered weaknesses before but need to be examined now in light of the immense personal requirements necessary for success as a business owner and leader.

LIST YOUR WEAKNESSES
(Own up to all of them.)

Now, go back and review your strengths and weaknesses. Compare your strengths and your alterable weaknesses with the characteristics common among successful entrepreneurs. Do you have significant weaknesses? If so, can most of them be positively changed? Do you think you have what it takes for entrepreneurial success?

Before embarking on any new enterprise, potential entrepreneurs need to be in touch with themselves, their desires and their personal objectives, as well as their strengths and weaknesses. The following format should help you become more aware of your individual goals and assist you in further assessing your personal qualities relative to the characteristics common among successful female entrepreneurs.

LIFE PLANNING

PURPOSE: TO SET AT LEAST TWO CLEAR GOALS FOR YOUR LIFE, TO SPECIFY PLANS OF ACTION TO REACH THOSE GOALS AND TO HELP YOU DETERMINE IF YOU HAVE A GENUINE INTEREST IN ENTREPRENEURSHIP.

Life Line

Use the following line to represent your life from beginning to end. Put a check mark on the line to indicate where you are now.

BIRTH_____**DEATH**

Address such questions as:

- What was the happiest year or period in your life?
- What was the turning point in your life?
- What was the lowest point in your life?

- Was there an event in your life when you demonstrated great courage?
- Was there a time of great grief?
- What peak experiences have you had? What things do you want to start doing at this point in your life?
- Was there a time when you were very enterprising?

Reflect on your feelings represented by the line before and after the check mark. What does this tell you about who you are and what you want out of life?

Typical Day

A circle will be used to depict how you spend a typical day. Divide the circle into four quarters using dotted lines. Each slice represents six hours. Now, estimate how many hours or parts of an hour you spend on each of the following areas on a typical day: SLEEP, SCHOOL, WORK, WITH FRIENDS--socializing, playing sports, etc., WITH FAMILY, ALONE--thinking, playing, reading, watching television, CHORES, MISCELLANEOUS PASTIMES, ETC.

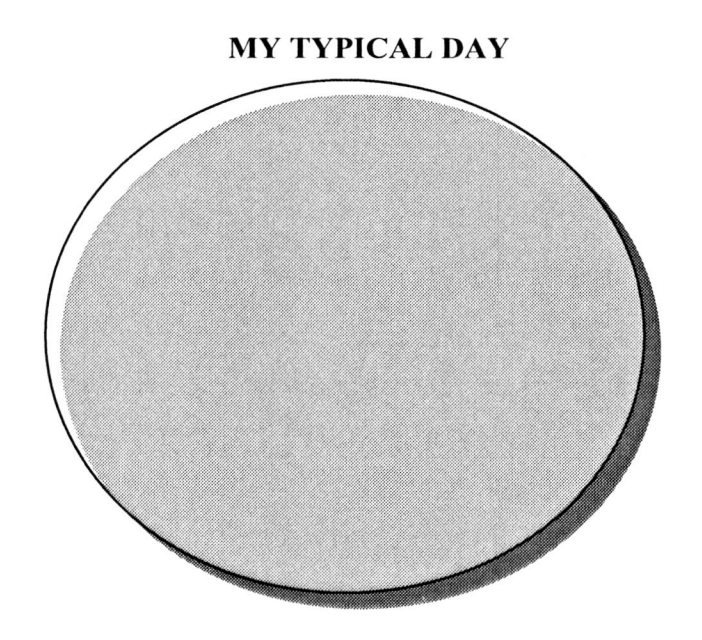

MY TYPICAL DAY

Are you satisfied with the relative sizes of your slices?

How Would You Like Your Ideal Day To Look?

Ideally, how big would you want each slice to be? Draw your ideal pie.

MY IDEAL DAY

Realistically, is there anything you can do to begin to change the size of some of your slices to the desired sizes?

SHORT-TERM AND LONG-TERM GOALS

What type of business do you see yourself running? What type of facility? How many employees do you have? How many customers or clients on a daily and monthly basis? What type of revenue and profit do you expect to realize in the beginning as well as subsequent years? What type of lifestyle do you want to create? At the same time, consider how much time will be required to achieve your goals? How much work will be required? Will your family be supportive or will conflicts arise? Sometimes you even need to consider subconscious jealousy and/or competition from your spouse or significant other and the negative repercussions. You may also run into the double bind of taking so much of your time to make your business a success and achieving the income that comes along with success that when you realize the fruits of your labor and have extra money to enjoy life through vacations and family fun, you don't have time to really enjoy yourself because you have to constantly devote more time to keeping the business successful, and/or you find that your mind is constantly on the business. This is one of the drawbacks of success. In essence, when you consider your goals, you may want to consciously limit your growth, based on your values, priorities and personal situation. This is a major consideration that should be addressed at the initiation of a business.

Make sure that you set realistic goals and expectations of yourself and your business. If your goals are too high, you will quickly find yourself discouraged and frustrated. Conservative business goals will allow you to be exuberant and more motivated when you do better than you anticipated. Make sure you have prioritized your goals, assessed all drawbacks and know what really makes you happy. Consider all of these factors as we proceed to the next section concerning the selection of a business that's right for you. But first take some time and write down your short-term and long-term goals. Make sure you attach a specific time frame to each goal.

SHORT-TERM GOALS

LONG-TERM GOALS

SELF-AWARENESS

This section involves looking at yourself by way of developing a coat of arms as seen on the following page. This should help you address the following considerations: WHAT AM I DOING WITH MY LIFE? AM I JUST REACTING TO OTHERS, OR AM I IN CONTROL OF THE DIRECTION OF MY LIFE? IS MY LIFE MAKING A DIFFERENCE? AM I JUST SETTLING FOR WHATEVER COMES MY WAY?

Answer each of the questions below by drawing in the appropriate area on the coat of arms on the following page. Use pictures, designs or symbols. Do not use words except in area six.

1. What do you regard as your greatest personal achievement to date?

2. What do you regard as your family's greatest achievement?

3. What do you regard as your own greatest personal failure to date?

4. What is something you are striving to become or to be?

5. What one thing would you want to accomplish by the time you are 85?

6. What is the personal motto by which you live?

COAT OF ARMS

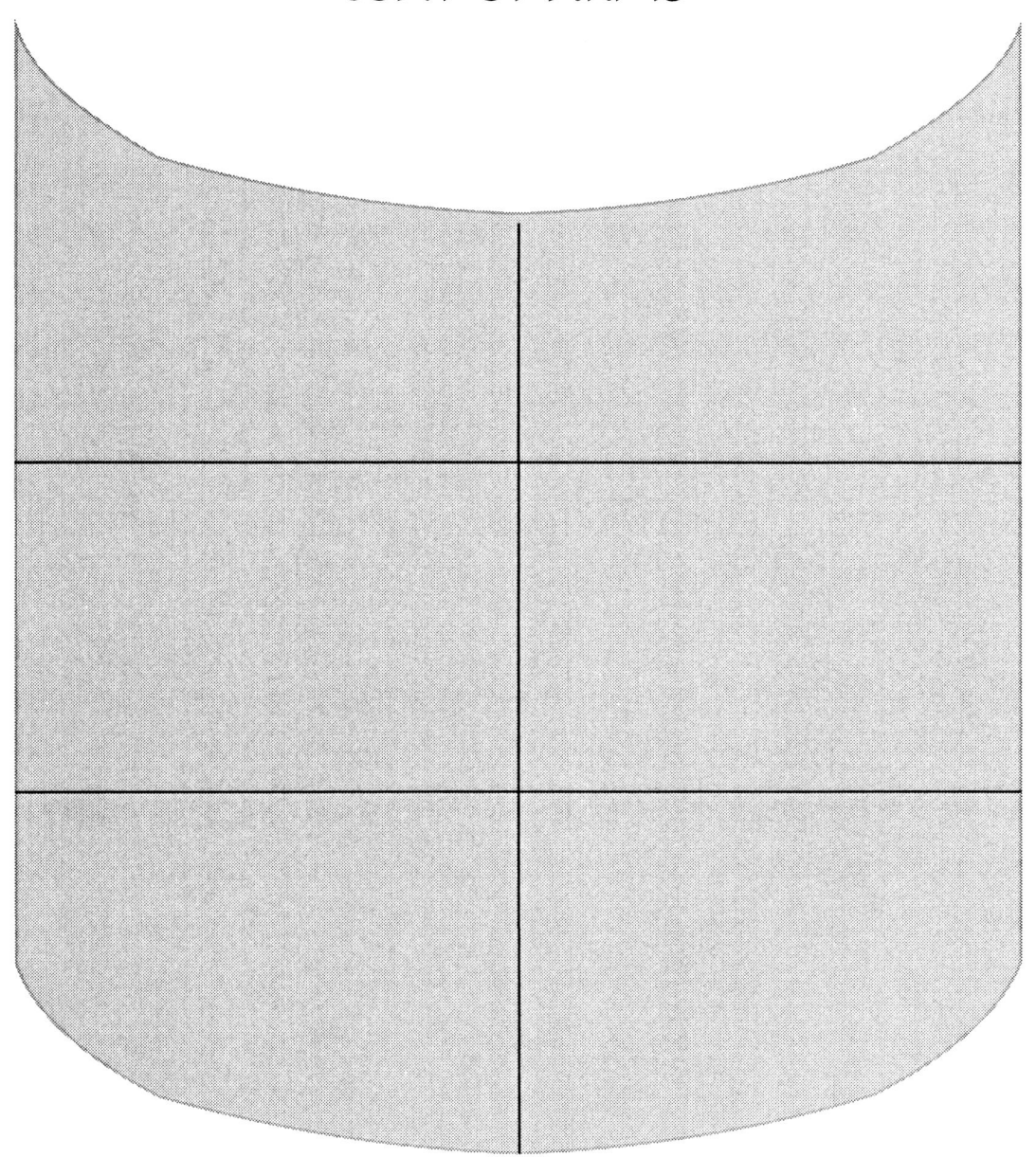

What would you most like to accomplish in your lifetime?

Write for two minutes without stopping. (Make sure to reflect on all aspects of your life including family, finances and the physical, social, spiritual, love and intellectual components of your life.)

You will need to thoroughly assess your likes and dislikes about work. The total responsibility of the business rests on the shoulders of the business owner. The business owner will need to be prepared to do all of the tasks required to keep the business going. Even though you may hire people to do the tasks you might dislike, such as bookkeeping, there will come a time when you will have to pitch in and help or do it all, either because of employee absence from work or because of cost-cutting considerations. In the beginning, you may be working with limited capital and may have to do everything yourself. Make sure that you are mentally prepared to cope with having to perform "hated" tasks.

LIKES AND DISLIKES ABOUT JOBS/WORK

LIKES	DISLIKES
1.	1.
2.	2.
3.	3.
4.	4.
5.	5.
6.	6.
7.	7.

REVIEW

Look back over your responses and address the following:

1. What do you want in your future?

2. You may find that priorities for your desires and goals have emerged. Set dates for accomplishments. You may have discovered hidden interests. Include the type of business you may want to start if it is part of your desires.

3. How do your personal characteristics rate compared to those of successful entrepreneurs?

HOW DO YOU PLAN TO GET THERE?

1. What resources do you have to help you achieve these goals?

2. What training or experience is needed to achieve these goals?

3. What things do you want or need to start doing less? More?

4. Are your life goals oriented toward owning and operating your own business? What type? What leads you to your conclusions?

SELECTING THE TYPE OF BUSINESS TO ENTER

Even though the number of female-owned businesses is increasing, the success of these ventures is not guaranteed. Successful ventures can only occur with careful planning and the execution of good business and management principles and practices, coupled with the existence of necessary personal factors on the part of the business owner.

Approximately 55 percent of all small business failures are due partially, if not entirely, to the lack of managerial ability and experience.[17] Certainly, therefore, managerial knowledge and ability are necessary for success in small business. This publication will provide the basic knowledge necessary for starting and operating a small business. It should be noted that management ability includes the personal requirements necessary for success which can often be overlooked when evaluating the reason a certain business is successful or unsuccessful. Entrepreneurial success depends significantly on the existence of strong personal entrepreneurial requirements and not business knowledge alone. This publication, therefore, also presents significant information concerning entrepreneurial characteristics as well as managerial knowledge. The information presented allows the reader to identify a type of business venture and then conduct an analysis to determine whether that possible business is, in fact, a feasible venture and whether it has a chance for success. At the same time, the information also allows the reader to develop a business plan for the venture.

BACKGROUND

There is not any consistent definition for a small business. Some of the small business literature uses a definition such as a firm having a name, an owner and one or more workers other than the owner. Using such a broad definition, approximately 95 percent of all businesses can be considered small. The Small Business Administration (SBA), the governmental agency directing efforts toward small business, defines a small business as a business independently owned and operated, and not dominant in its field. The SBA goes further to categorize firms as being small by way of certain criteria such as number of employees and dollar volume of business. One really has to develop a feel for what a small business is. Generally, if one is starting a new business, it can be assumed that it will be considered small initially. Small business offers many benefits. Small firms tend to:

1. be more in touch with employees, thereby encouraging better employee relations;
2. be more in touch with customers and can provide more personal service;
3. provide almost half of all jobs;
4. help insure competition;
5. provide jobs for the disadvantaged and ethnic groups;
6. help expand the economy;
7. provide workers and owners with wider learning experiences;
8. provide personal rewards (i.e., financial security or wealth, personal satisfaction and, what is considered a major advantage by many, independence).

The problems encountered by small businesses are many. The disadvantages and pitfalls of small business include the following:

1. Fewer opportunities to make costly mistakes (One major mistake such as purchasing the wrong inventory can cause failure.),
2. Inadequate funds to employ managerial assistance or consulting help,
3. Shortage of working capital,
4. Poor record-keeping systems,
5. Lack of effective selling techniques,
6. No marketing research,
7. Inability to cope with growth problems,
8. Lack of experience of many entrepreneurs,
9. Poor location selection,
10. Too much inventory, particularly the wrong kind,
11. Excessive purchase of fixed assets, such as elaborate buildings when first starting,
12. Poor credit-granting policies,
13. Unwarranted personal expenditures;
14. Unplanned expansions.

Given the many pitfalls of small business, the failure rate of small businesses is extraordinarily high. Half of the businesses started each year fail. Half of the businesses that fail, do so during the first five years of operation. Nine out of ten failures are traceable to managerial inexperience and incompetence. Other reasons for business failures include too little capital, poor organization, obsolescence of service or product, obsolescence of equipment, poor personnel practices, and inappropriate personal characteristics.

At this point, I hope you have determined that you have or can develop the personal characteristics required for success as an entrepreneur and that you truly want to take the entrepreneurial challenge. We now need to put those success traits into action and start developing your business.

Types of Businesses

By virtue of the fact that you are reading this book, you have probably already decided that you want to start a child care business or some type of business caring for young people. The type of business you enter will be influenced by your personal value system, education, training, financial ability and family situation, as well as by your particular interests and desires.

Small businesses can be categorized into six types:

1. retailing,
2. service,
3. wholesaling,
4. research and development,
5. consulting, and
6. manufacturing.

You must start with a business idea and develop your business or venture from there. Before making a preliminary analysis of the market, production or financial aspects of your venture, you must be able to describe and define your business concept. An idea for a business must address a need of an identified market which is presently not satisfied and, at the same time, be innovative enough to attract people to your product or service as opposed to the competition. It is important to be innovative enough to attract customers; but if your service or product is too unique, it may take too long for people to accept it, and your business will fail while you attempt to make people aware of the need for your product or service. Realize that the type of business you enter will be influenced by your personal value system, education, training, financial ability and your family situation, as well as by your particular interests and desires. As you attempt to think of the type of business you may want to start, reflecting on the following list of some specific types of businesses may trigger a few thoughts. The list is presented only to serve as a "bouncing board."

Antique shop
Art show promotion
Artwork (sales)
Baby-sitting service (day-night)
Bake shop
Beauty services
Business consulting
Calligraphy instruction
Candy-making business
Caning chairs
Child care
Classes and instruction in your skill areas
Casket rental
Cleaning services
Clown birthday party service
Computer sales
Consignment shop (clothier, baby items, furniture)
Craft shop
Day care
Dietary bakery
Disco
Designer clothier (boutique, rentals, re-sale)
Dinners to go (elegant take-out dinners or healthy dinners)

Elder care
Errand service
Fabric sales and design
Financial services
Flowers and plants (preservation services, arrangement, rentals)
Food service (delivery, different homemade items, catering)
Frame shop (sales, framing, unique design)
Fur sales
Furniture sales and rental
Gifts (sales, buying, wrapping and delivery service)
Gourmet coffee and tea shop
Greenhouses (sales, installation, consultation on use)
Herb shop
Instruction (piano, gymnastics, dancing, etc.)
Jewelry
Lawn care service (grass cutting, plant, flower and shrub planting and care)
Legal courier service
Maid service
Manufacturing
Monogram service
Movie club
Nannies for rent
Oriental rugs
Pet grooming and care
Potato restaurant
Public relations firm
Roller skating rink
Roommate finder service
Sale-by-owner listing (listing of homes for sale by owners)
Salads only restaurant
Sick child child care
Silk flower rental service
Self-service pet wash (like a car wash for animals)
Security patrol service
Telephone answering service
Secretarial service
Temporary personnel service
Tennis/Racquetball club
Tourist services
Video gameroom

In selecting a business you should address the following major questions:

1. What type of business do you think you might want to enter? Why?

2. Exactly what products and/or services should be sold?

3. Who will be the primary customer groups for your product or service?

4. What are the eventual uses for your product or service by the customer?

5. Why will customers want to buy your product or service? (Ask yourself questions such as what are the key benefits or advantages of your product or service to the customer: lower price, quality, etc.?)

6. What in fact is your total product? (List everything you will be offering to your customers, not only the physical.)

ASSESSING YOUR MONETARY REQUIREMENTS

The question that is probably running through your mind is how much money is needed to get the business started and keep it operating? This question cannot be addressed without first taking an in-depth look at the total venture you're considering. All of the information obtained can then be compiled in a business plan format. Below you will find factors that will need to be addressed and considered in determining start-up and operating costs. This information is presented in brief in this section. It is presented at this time so that you will be conscious of significant cost centers as we begin working on preparing a business plan for your venture. Capital requirements will be addressed in a more detailed worksheet format as a part of the business plan preparation process in Chapter III.

The amount of money you will need to start your business depends on many factors. The following are major factors you need to take into consideration in determining your monetary requirements:

- the type of business being established,
- the location of the business,
- the sales volume anticipated to be obtained,
- how quickly the sales volume desired can be obtained,
- whether you buy or lease the facilities in which the business will be operating,
- how extensive the product line is,
- whether the business will operate on a cash basis or extend credit,

- how much money the entrepreneur has to invest in the business,
- whether legal assistance is needed,
- the cost of preparing the business facility for use,
- the cost of store fixtures and equipment,
- the amount and cost of the starting inventory,
- the cost of establishing an accounting system and the forms required,
- the cost of personnel,
- the cost of delivering merchandise to customers and inventory to the business,
- the cost of licenses and permits,
- the cost of utilities,
- the cost of insurance,
- advertising expenses, and
- the amount of money deposited in a reserve fund to take care of business and personal expenses until your business gets going.

All of these factors have been taken into consideration in the preparation of the cost worksheets that follow. As we work on the preparation of your business plan, you will be able to insert certain costs when they are considered.

START-UP COSTS

Start-up costs include all of the expenses your business will incur in preparation for opening. Major cost areas are presented below; however, you will need to alter the sample form based on the specifics of your business. Some of the expenses listed will be one-time only costs or expenses you incur once a year. Other expenses will occur monthly.

BUSINESS ORGANIZATIONAL EXPENSES	MONTHLY	YEARLY
Start-up inventory		
Facility costs		
Decorating and remodeling		
Furniture		
Professional and legal fees		
Franchise fee, if applicable		
Licenses and permits		
Telephone installation		
Telephone services		
Telephone answering service		
Insurance		
Personnel		
Deposits for utilities		
Installation of fixtures		
TOTAL		
ADVERTISING AND PROMOTIONAL EXPENSES		
Business cards		
Mailers, posters, ads		
Business logo design		
Signs (outdoor)		
Bags		
Other		
TOTAL		
OFFICE OPERATING EXPENSES		
Stationery		

Invoice forms		
Purchase order forms		
Computer		
Pens, pencils, misc.		
Tables & Equipment		
Other		
TOTAL		
FURNITURE AND FIXTURES		
Desks and chairs		
Filing cabinets		
Wastebaskets		
Safe		
Copying machine		
Adding machine		
Storage shelves		
Cabinets		
Computers & Technology		
Office furniture		
Lighting		
Toy storage		
Bookcases		
TOTAL		
BUSINESS VEHICLE		
REAL ESTATE		
EQUIPMENT		
OWNER'S LIVING EXPENSES		
Home mortgage payments or rent		
Food		
Home repair and maintenance		
Outstanding debts (Credit cards, etc,)		
Loans		
Entertainment		
Education		
Auto and repair		
Furniture		
Clothing		
Travel		
Taxes		
Utilities		
Medical expenses		
Insurance costs		
Other		

TOTAL		
TOTAL PERSONAL EXPENSES		
Subtract outside income to still be obtained while running business.		
TOTAL PERSONAL EXPENSES TO BE COVERED BY THE BUSINESS		

EVALUATING YOUR MONETARY REQUIREMENTS

Prior to approaching a lending institution or investors for assistance in funding your business, you will need to make sure you have the answers to the following questions:

1. How much money do you need?

2. What exactly do you need the money for? Some specific reasons for needing money include buying equipment, supplies, renting space, salaries, money to meet financial obligations to suppliers, etc.

3. What collateral do you have? What do you or your business own which can be offered as security for money received?

4. When do you need the money?

5. How long do you need the money?

6. Can you afford the cost of the money?

7. Where can you find the money? (Make sure you have backups in place.)

REMEMBER IT IS BETTER TO OVERESTIMATE THAN UNDERESTIMATE YOUR FINANCIAL REQUIREMENTS!!

The answers to all of these questions and other major business considerations should be summarized in a coherent, precise written format. This information constitutes a business plan and is discussed in the following chapter.

CHAPTER III

The Business Plan

"Three Critical Keys to Entrepreneurial Success:

PASSION, PLANNING AND PERSEVERANCE."

M.G.L.J.

THE BUSINESS PLAN

A business plan is a report written by the initiator of a business which describes the venture in detail--WHAT business you are in, WHO will be active in it, WHY you believe it will be successful, and HOW you intend to implement your plans. The business plan should be prepared with great care and thought and should be concise, readable, well written, and substantive.

From an internal perspective, the business plan forces the business owner to write down all of his or her thoughts and researched data pertaining to the business. Many considerations would go unaddressed, and many thoughts and ideas would never be captured again if it were not for the business plan. The business plan is also crucial because it serves as a checklist and timetable for accomplishing stated objectives.

Externally, the business plan is used to attract financial as well as human resources. Lending institutions and investors want to be able to examine your organized plans to determine if your venture has merit and whether it warrants their investment. The business plan can also be used to attract key personnel and business partners, as well as serve as a means to communicate to others what your business is about. Even many small business consulting firms and assistance offices will ask you for a business plan prior to rendering any type of service. A GOOD BUSINESS PLAN IS CRUCIAL!

A good business plan will consist of, but is not limited to, the following major informational areas.

The Business

- Detailed description of the business including name, location, business goals and objectives, industry information and assessment, economic trends, etc.;

- Description of the product (services and/or goods), potential of product line, technology, and possible advances;

- Description of the marketing plan including target market, marketing strategies, channels of distribution, market size and share, market potential, pricing strategy, and promotion;

- Assessment of competition;

- Management covering such areas as key personnel, names of accountants, lawyers, consultants, organizational structure, experience of key personnel, educational background and experience;

- Legal structure describing the proprietorship, partnership, or corporation;

- Personnel, listing personnel requirements, position descriptions, labor trends, and compensation;

- Facilities and equipment;

- Sources of supply;

- Critical risks and problems;

- Economic trends; and

- Strategies for the future.

Financial Data

- Capital equipment,
- Sources of funds,
- Balance sheet,
- Break-even analysis,
- Income projections or profit-loss statement,
- Pro forma cash flow,
- Uses of funds, and
- Desired funding.

Supporting Documents

- Resumes of key personnel,
- Personal financial statements,
- Credit reports,
- Letters of reference,
- Copies of leases,
- Contracts,
- Legal documents,
- Drawings,
- Photographs,
- Articles, and

- Any additional pertinent information.

The following worksheets are provided to help you organize your thoughts regarding your business. The remaining format of this publication will present crucial information necessary for starting a small child care business followed by questions for you to address. The summarization of the answers to these questions will be important components of your business plan. Upon completion of this publication, you should have your business plan in good order.

Now that you have a feel for what is included in a completed business plan, continue reading the next chapter on start-up costs. It will become obvious that in order to fill in most of these blanks, substantial investigatory work will have to be done on your part. In fact, these blanks will need to be filled in, as well as the questions answered from the previous section on your financial needs, before you near the completion of your plan. All of these questions need to be kept in mind throughout the business plan preparation process.

BUSINESS PLAN WORKSHEETS

The importance of a well-conceived business plan cannot be stressed enough. The business plan outline covers the major topics to be considered in the planning process. Experience has revealed that most mistakes or failures of businesses occur not from bad information, but from a lack of information. The business plan, among other things, helps you to determine if you have sufficient information, capital and customers to initiate your venture.

As stated earlier, the business plan is of immense importance in requesting a bank loan or any form of financing or assistance. Even an advertising consultant will ask to see your business plan before attempting to map out an advertising program for your firm. These worksheets are designed in such a way that you can simply fill in the blanks and have a basic narrative for all business plan components. As you proceed with this manual, insert the appropriate information in the spaces provided. Also, make sure you insert appropriate costs on your cost sheets. Upon completion of the publication, you should have completed your business plan and have it ready to be typed.

BUSINESS PLAN

NAME OF THE BUSINESS: _____

Be sure the name is distinctive, will stick in the minds of your customers or clients, and is accurately descriptive of the nature of your business. Also check to make sure that no one else is using the name or a very similar name, particularly in the same industry.

Check with your state trademark office and register your business name. This is usually not very expensive, but be sure to include the cost on your cost sheet. You may also want to register your business name and logo, that is, the symbol that you use to identify your business, with the Federal Trademark Office. If you are having trouble coming up with a name, don't belabor the point. A good name will probably come to you as you continue your investigatory work into the industry.

LOCATION: In light of the selected target market and after reflecting on many major location considerations, _____ will be strategically
(name of business)

located at:_____.

This location was selected because.........

Take time to thoroughly assess your location options and reflect on the information presented in this section of the manual. Make sure you have considered such factors as the pros and cons of a post office box, your business image, operating out of a home office, and accessibility to your target market, as well as cost factors. (See Chapter VI.)

TELEPHONE: _____

Make sure you have a business listing in the phone book even if you are operating out of the home. Your accessibility by phone is very important. If you cannot afford a secretary, use an answering service. Avoid answering machines if at all possible. They are a turn-off to most people. Don't forget to include your business telephone and answering service costs on your cost sheets.

STATEMENT OF PURPOSE AND NATURE OF BUSINESS:

_____

_____

_____

WHAT IS THE PURPOSE OF YOUR BUSINESS? WHAT MARKET ARE YOU AIMING FOR? WHY ARE YOU IN BUSINESS? THIS SHOULD BE A SUCCINCT STATEMENT PERTAINING TO WHAT YOUR BUSINESS IS ALL ABOUT.

EXAMPLE: "A BUSINESS OF YOUR OWN" is a multi-faceted service firm established to assist women in starting and managing small businesses. "A BUSINESS OF YOUR OWN" specializes in business start-up publications and auxiliary services to assist the female small business owner and aspiring owner. "A BUSINESS OF YOUR OWN" publications range from general start-up manuals to more specific manuals with information about starting particular businesses. "A BUSINESS OF YOUR OWN'S" goal is to assist women in pulling together the intricate components necessary to make their small businesses successful.

Industry Overview: Examine the industry your business is in from national, regional and local standpoints. Include a narrative which will address historical and concrete growth projections along with the number of firms locally and nationally. Discuss how your venture fits into the industry context and indicate factors that will give your business the competitive edge in the marketplace based on industry information. Much industry information can be obtained from the local library, trade associations and trade publications and from websites. Be sure to check the appendix of this manual for useful informational sources.

Form of Ownership: _____ is a _____.
   name of business   form of ownership

Discuss the form of legal ownership (proprietorship, partnership, or corporation) your business will use and why. (See Chapter V.)

Marketing: Discuss your **target market**. Use results from your research to justify the appropriateness of your market. Cite published information which support your target market selection. Discuss in detail your "total product," including auxiliary services, packaging, warranties, delivery service, repairs, installation, guarantees, etc. Detail your promotion plans for attracting customers or clients, penetrating your target market, and getting repeat customers. Again, do not forget to insert all of your marketing costs on the cost sheets. Discuss how your product will be **distributed** and/or how services will be performed. What type of market penetration do you hope to obtain and when? What is the **pricing** structure for your products and services? Make sure you can show legitimate justification for all of your business decisions and make sure you are being consistent with your image and product positioning. (See Chapter IV.)

The selected target market for _____
                                (name of business)

is _____. This market was determined
   (target market)

to be appropriate after conducting marketing research. _____ individuals were surveyed
                                                        (# people)

for the purpose of _____ and to determine if originally identified target market would be receptive to the business idea. The survey findings are presented in the appendix.

The product of _____ is presently in the
(name of business)

_____ stage of development. The product has many
(introduction, growth, maturity)

strengths including _____. In spite of the many strengths of the business's products/services, certain weaknesses have been identified. These weaknesses are as follows: _____. The identified weaknesses will be overcome by _____
(action to be taken)
_____.

To inform and persuade customers/clients to patronize _____,
(name of business)

a varied promotional strategy name of business will be employed. This strategy will include
_____
(types of promotion)

Distribution of the product or service will be achieved by _____.

A _____ pricing strategy will be used. This was decided because
(penetration/skimming)
_____
_____.

Competition: The strengths of the competition date will be overcome by……...WHO ARE YOUR MAJOR COMPETITORS? WHAT SHARE OF THE MARKET DO THEY

PRESENTLY HAVE? WHAT ARE THEIR STRENGTHS AND WEAKNESSES? HOW WILL YOU OVERCOME THEIR STRENGTHS AND OBTAIN A VIABLE SHARE OF THE MARKET? WHAT SHARE OF THE MARKET DO YOU HOPE TO OBTAIN AND WHEN?

Research indicated that there are _____ major immediate competitors.
(# of competitors)

The major competitors are: _____,

_____, _____,

_____ and _____.

They have _____, _____, _____ and _____ percent shares of the market respectively.

COMPETITOR ANALYSIS

Competitor Name	Strengths	Weaknesses

Personnel: Discuss all of your personnel requirements. Discuss all of the activities that will be necessary in order for your firm to accomplish its objectives, and then discuss the type of people you plan to hire to carry out these activities. Make sure to address qualifications, compensation plans and any other major personnel considerations. Discuss the <u>key management personnel</u> with particular attention being paid to their experience in the industry and their qualifications. Attach resumes for all key personnel. Devote a separate section to addressing the qualifications of the business owner. Don't fail to include a narrative about your success qualities which were discussed and assessed earlier in this manual.

Initially, _____ will have _____.
                 (name of business)   (# employees)

They will hold the following positions and have the following responsibilities:

Positions	Responsibilities

Personnel will be compensated based on _____.

Key Personnel: The key personnel are (include yourself):

Their qualifications and functions are as follows:

Position	Qualifications	Functions

Organizational Structure: After you have determined the types of activities necessary to fulfill your organization's objectives, you can determine the most logical way for these activities to interact within the confines of the organization. Who does what? Who is accountable to whom? Diagram your organizational structure. Initially, the organizational structure may only consist of you, but think about growth planning.

Production: Describe the facilities necessary to house the operations of your business. Discuss any lease or purchase arrangements and all facility improvement plans along with costs for these arrangements and plans. Re-examine the rationale for your selection of the facility and the lease or purchase decision.

If you are producing a product or service, discuss production in detail. Address inventory and quality control considerations as well as costs.

Facilities:

Initially, _____ will be housed in _____.
             (name of business)   (describe facility)

The facility consists of. . . . .

Equipment:

Explain in detail and list all required equipment, fixtures, etc. Assess the costs and discuss the purchase and lease arrangements and payment terms.

Supplies:

List all of your supply requirements including the names of the suppliers and the terms of payment. Assess the reasoning behind the selection of a supplier. Include delivery time, order quantities and backup sources for all supplies. (See Chapter XII.)

Insurance:

List insurance coverage to be carried on your business facility, equipment, officers and liability coverage.

Accounting Firm:

Discuss your selection of an accounting firm, the services they will be performing and the costs for these services. Include the address of the accounting firm.

The business will use the accounting services of _____.
                                                           (name of accounting firm)

Their services have been obtained because _____.

They will provide the following services _____.

Banks/Financial Institutions:

_____

_____

_____

Legal Counsel:

Discuss services to be performed and costs.

_____

_____

_____

Critical Risks and Problems:

_____

_____

_____

Growth Plans:

_____

_____

_____

_____

Financial Information:

The next step is to translate your business plan into dollars. Make sure to include profit/loss forecasts, pro forma balance sheets, cash flow projections and break-even analysis.

Make sure that you have inserted all of the pertinent cost information on your cost sheets and that you have transferred them to the appropriate financial statements. Thoroughly assess your capital requirements necessary to get your business off the ground and running for at least one year.

Appendix:

Provide Support Documentation Including, But Not Limited To, The Following:

- Resumes of Key Personnel
- Personal Financial Statements
- Credit Reports
- Letters of Reference
- Copies of Leases (if applicable)
- Contracts (if applicable)
- Legal Documents
- Insurance Policies
- Partnership Agreements or Corporation Charter (if applicable)
- Patents
- Copyrights
- Trademarks
- Buy/Sell Contract
- Promotional Material

- Photographs (if deemed appropriate)
- Brochures

CHAPTER IV

Marketing

"The entrepreneur is a walking and talking billboard for her business. You must present a professional appearance at all times, even in the grocery store."

M.G.L.J.

MARKETING

Regardless of the type of business one selects to start, there will be a product or service that needs to be sold or marketed to the public. Contrary to old beliefs of production orientation where firms decided what they wanted to make and then attempted to sell the product, it is advisable for firms to adhere to the marketing orientation concept. This concept holds that firms should seek to satisfy their customers at a profit. This involves determining the needs and wants of a selected customer group first, and then attempting to satisfy their desires. Encompassed here is the selection of a target market, a group of individuals to whom you want to direct your efforts and attempt to satisfy, followed by the manipulation of what is called the marketing mix to satisfy this target market. The **marketing mix** (or the 4 P's), include the **product, price, place,** and **promotion**. In other words, you must come up with the right product, at the right price, at the right place and use the right promotion to satisfy the chosen target market. The "four P's" are explained in the following sections.

Product

The product component of the marketing mix includes not only the specific good or service offered for sale, but its reputation, name, packaging, image, as well as accompanying services and innovative services such as incorporating foreign language into the learning program. The product of a business, in fact, does not have to be physical at all but could be the rendering of a type of service such as medical care or child care.

Therefore, the total product offered by a firm may include a large array of goods as well as related services such as parking facilities and credit. Total product planning is obviously crucial in order to provide the "right" product for the selected target market. Total product planning needs to encompass cognition of product life cycles. Like humans, products go through life cycles. The life cycle of products is generally divided into several stages: product introduction, market growth, market maturity, sales decline, and termination.

The **introduction stage** involves informing the target market of the existence of the product or service as well as its advantages and uses. During the introductory stage a great deal of money is spent on promoting the product. The business may experience losses since money is invested in the business at this point for future benefits.

During the **growth stage**, the business owner will begin to make a profit. As other firms or individuals see the entrepreneur making money, some will try to imitate the product. Competition, therefore, becomes strong during this phase.

During the **market maturity stage**, many competitors have entered the market. Competition may be very fierce and could cause profits to decline. Advertising, thus, becomes very important. This phase, as well as the other stages, could last for any period of time.

During the **sales decline phase**, new products begin to replace the old. If a firm sees its "total" product moving into the sales decline phase, intense planning needs to be conducted to alter the product or even change products or the nature of the business before sales decline significantly. However, product planning needs to be conducted continuously so as to avoid getting into the sales decline predicament. Entrepreneurs must be ever conscious of their environment to be prepared to change direction or alter strategies and/or products quickly.

The **termination phase** involves the termination of product sales because a market no longer exists for the product, or the product is obsolete because of new technological advances or alternative choices formerly not available.

Surveying the Market for Product Marketability

You need to see if your perception of the need for your product or service is the same as your identified customer group or target market which you wish to serve. At this point, an interview of constituents in your target market should be conducted to see if your identified customer group desires your product or service, or whether your business idea is satisfying any need except your need to be in business for yourself.

A brief questionnaire should be drawn up and presented either verbally or in written form. Questions should be designed to give you specific answers, but at the same time open enough for respondents to possibly give you some ideas for product or service improvement when they respond. The sample questionnaire which follows should serve as a guide in designing a survey for your business idea. Be sure to survey as many individuals as possible who are in your target market.

Sample Questionnaire
(Designed for An Oral Interview)

We are surveying the market for child care services and would appreciate your assistance in providing the following information.

1. Do you have children requiring child care? If yes, please indicate their age(s).

2. Are you presently looking for any particular child care services? If yes, what type?

3. Where have you previously taken your child for child care? Were you satisfied with the services of this establishment?

4. What features would make a child care center particularly attractive to you? (e.g., foreign language education)

5. What major factors would determine whether you chose a child care center?

6. During what hours of the day would you desire child care?

7. Please indicate the days of the week you will need child care?

8. Would you desire drop-in service? If yes, indicate days of the week, time, and how often.

9. Please provide the following information about yourself.

   Sex ____M ____F

   Race _____

   Married ____ **Single** ____

Household income range:

under $30,000 _____

$30,000-49,000 _____

$50,000-69,000 _____

$70,000-89,000 _____

above $90,000 _____

Rent _____   Own Home _____

10. Section of city where you reside: _____

11. Section of city where you work: _____

12. Section of city that would be most convenient for a child care service:_____

Evaluate your questionnaire responses. Is your service desired by your target market as a result of the information received from the questionnaire? Does your target market need to be changed or widened? Does your total service/product need changing?

It must now be determined whether the service offered is technically feasible, whether it could achieve a competitive advantage, and if the cost and time necessary for development are worthwhile.

A. <u>Status</u>

   1. What is the current stage of development of the venture's service (introduction, maturity, etc.)? Is there something that gives your service a "new twist" in the minds of the public?

If the service needs licenses, indicate which ones and all the procedures necessary for obtaining them. Also indicate all permits or certificates as applicable.

2. What must be done to get the service ready for sale? Think in terms of the total product and packaging.

B. Strengths and Weaknesses

Strengths

1. Indicate any patents or trade secrets on your service. Do these give you a competitive advantage?

2. What design features of your service give it an advantage over the competition?

3. What is your estimate of the life expectancy of your service?

Weaknesses

1. Are there any features of your service that may put it at a disadvantage in the marketplace?

2. Indicate any possibilities of rapid change in demand because of population trends and/or developments such as an increased number of corporate child care centers or after school care provided by your school system.

Price

Price is another one of the "four P's" which the entrepreneur can adjust to satisfy the target market. A pricing strategy must be developed. The entrepreneur must determine whether products generally will be priced higher, lower, or the same as the competition. Initially, the products could be offered at a price lower than the competition's to obtain a high sales volume, with prices raised later **(penetration pricing)**, or the products could be offered initially at a high price and lowered later **(skimming pricing)**. The entrepreneur also has the task of determining the specific price of all products and/or services. With pricing the product or service, there are many factors to consider. Included are: channel of distribution used, competition's pricing strategy, annual anticipated sales volume, product life cycle, opportunity for special promotions, the image of the product, and operation expenses.

Place

The determination of the appropriate channel of distribution to use for the product to get to the target market is a major part of place considerations. There are four basic channels of distribution that the entrepreneur may want to consider, and of course, there are many variations of the four. For child care centers, location is a major factor considered here. Of course, a child care center should be located in a geographic area that is convenient to your target market and safe for children.

Promotion

Promotion involves persuading the target market to purchase your product or service. Sales promotion can use either direct or indirect methods. Direct promotion methods include advertising, publicity, displays, special event sales, and personal selling; whereas, indirect promotion methods include public relations, customer relations, customer services, and product packaging. Another part of promotion is advertising. For the new firm, advertising is particularly important because new or potential customers must be made aware of the firm's existence. Even though word-of-mouth advertising is fine and, in fact, crucial, a firm cannot rely solely on this form of advertising. Small business people need to incorporate advertising costs into their budgets, allocating monthly amounts in this area. To be successful, advertising must be consistent, image building, and continuous. The new entrepreneur needs to start off with advertising which will bring immediate action (i.e., immediate response ads).

There are a variety of advertising media which can be used.

- Newspapers
- Magazines
- Radio
- Direct Mail
- Television
- Web Sites
- Point-of-Purchase Displays
- Bench Advertising

- Billboards
- Motion Advertising (public transportation)
- Fliers and Brochures
- Speciality Items or Novelty Items (such as pens, calendars, etc.)
- Free Publicity
- Telephone Yellow Pages

The selection of the best media for a small firm is not an easy endeavor. Television is not appropriate for most small firms due to the cost factor and the probability that you may be reaching many individuals who are not in your target market, thus you are incurring unnecessary costs. Large newspapers also tend to be quite expensive. Local or community papers also tend to be somewhat expensive; however, local or community papers may be a viable option. Magazines also tend to be costly, and with the exception of local magazines, may cover too much territory for a small business. Advertising spots on a local radio station may be feasible if the costs are in line and you can get the most advantageous time for reaching your target market.

Billboards often are effective near the location of the business but also are costly. Speciality advertisement, which includes calendars, rain scarves and pens, tends to be effective and can be as costly or as inexpensive as you desire. Motion advertising tends to be effective if your market uses transportation such as buses, taxis, and subways on a routine basis. The use of the telephone book should not be overlooked, as many potential customers do pre-shopping by the phone. Direct-mail advertising is used by a great number of small businesses. It is less expensive than many other forms of advertising and provides the small business owner with selective coverage. Your child care center should consider having a website which would detail all of your services. A website is really a "must have" in the 21st Century.

The goal of advertising is to sell by way of the **"AIDA"** formula. This formula means you must get the potential customer's **attention**, make them **interested** in your product or service, create a **desire** for your product, and bring about **action**--the purchase of your product or service.

Basic Advertising Guidelines

1. **Start with the sales budget.**

   - Decide what percentage of your anticipated sales volume you will allocate to advertising. Use the following approach: research trade journals, estimate monthly sales, and consider special promotions.

2. **Profile yourself and your customers.**
   - What business am I in?
   - What quality of child care do I sell?
   - What kind of image do I want to project?
   - How do I compare with the competition?
   - What customer services do I offer?
   - What are my customers' tastes?
   - Why will they buy from me?

3. **Select the appropriate advertising media for your business.**

4. **Adhere to the following pointers for printed ads.**

    - Make ads easy to recognize.
    - Use simple layouts.
    - Use dominant illustrations to feature services.
    - Show the product's benefits to the reader.
    - State a price or range of prices.
    - Include the business name, address, phone number, e-mail address, and website.
    - Repeat an ad if the response is good.

5. **AIDA:** Get the customer's **attention,** arouse their **interest**, make them **desire** your product and finally, get them to take **action** or buy your product. This is the goal of advertising.

Measuring the Results of Advertising

There are different types of advertisements and different measuring methods. **Immediate-response** advertising is designed to cause the potential customer to buy a particular product from you within a short time. The following is a list of tests to measure the response to the advertisements.

- Coupons brought in,
- Requests by phone or letters referring to the ad,
- Sales made of a particular service, and

- Business traffic

Attitude advertising is the reputation or image builder form of advertising. To measure its effectiveness:

- Run an ad every week and compare each week's sales with the same week of the previous year, and
- Ask customers how they heard about your business

Marketing Research

Marketing research is essentially a systematic way of finding out general information pertaining to the marketing of one's own goods or services or learning about one's customers and/or competition. It assists one in determining who should be in the target market (group of people to whom you are addressing your efforts and trying to satisfy) and the demographic information and spending habits of those potential customers. In addition, it helps to verify whether you have the goods and/or services the customers want and whether the promotional strategy is appropriate and effective.

There are two major types of marketing research: **secondary** and **primary**. **Secondary** involves the utilization of published information such as: surveys, books and magazines. **Primary** research pertains to information obtained directly from one's target market. Primary research may take the form of a questionnaire (direct mail or personal), telephone surveys, test marketing, behavior observation, etc.

Marketing research does not have to be expensive because a great amount of the information can be gathered by the entrepreneur. License plates of cars in the parking area or neighborhood can provide an idea of where customers or potential customers live (county) so that advertising can be directed accordingly. Also, questionnaires can be utilized and the examination of telephone numbers given on a mailing list or personal check can provide an idea of the section of the city in which customers live. Coupons used in connection with radio ads requiring customers to mention a radio station's name to get a special discount will also help to determine who is hearing certain ads. Of course, an observant entrepreneur is necessary. Looking at how customers dress, whether they are married and/or have children, and what age, ethnic background, likes, dislikes, and what other characteristics they possess is also important.

Using some form of marketing research, the potential entrepreneur needs to estimate the approximate size of the total potential market.

Attempt to estimate your market size. Indicate sources of data for your approximation. Some of the references from the bibliography should be helpful here. The approximate size of my market is _____.

It is also necessary to thoroughly analyze your competition. A table such as the one that follows may be helpful with this endeavor.

TABLE I

Name and Address of Competitor	% Estimated Market Share	Estimated Yearly Sales $	Comments on Competitor's Strengths and Weaknesses

How can you overcome your competitors' strengths to gain a competitive edge?

What market share (% of the market) do you think you can acquire?

Marketing Tactics

1. What methods will you use to sell your service (direct selling, website, yellow pages, radio ads, etc.)?

2. What are your marketing strategies?

3. Will you offer unique services and/or specialized care services?

4. How will you bring your service to the attention of potential customers?

5. What type of advertising will you use?

6. How much will it cost and how long will it take to establish a market share for your service? (Make a rough estimate.)

Examining the Economic Environment of Your Business

The total environment in which your business will be operating must also be considered when determining an appropriate marketing strategy. As you thoroughly investigate the child care industry, keep in mind that the U.S. Census Bureau NAICS Code for Child Day Care Services is 624410. The SIC Code is 8351.

The following questions should be addressed.

1. How many firms are in this industry?

2. Do they vary in size?

3. Where are most of the enterprises located?

4. What is the relationship between small firms of this type and larger firms in the industry?

5. Do the firms serve English-speaking only or some bilingual markets?

6. What is the government's attitude toward this type of business?

7. What is society's attitude about your type of business or your industry?

8. What is the market for your business? Consider age, sex, education, birth rate, population trends, income, competition, etc. of your target market.

*"To be a successful entrepreneur you must be **results-oriented** and **resilient** with a keen understanding of the importance of **relationships** and **respec**t."*

M.G.L.J.

CHAPTER V

Forms of Business Ownership

" Look into the future with vision and vivaciously create a business climate based on values."

M.G.L.J.

FORMS OF BUSINESS OWNERSHIP

There are three major legal forms of business ownership: the **sole proprietorship**, **partnership** and **corporation**. One form cannot be said to be better than the other as one must consider the advantages and disadvantages of each in light of his or her needs and desires. Below, the three forms are evaluated in terms of their advantages and disadvantages.

Proprietorship

An enterprise owned by one individual is a **proprietorship**. The owner and the business are one and the same and cannot be legally distinguished and separated in the eyes of the law. This is the most common form of legal ownership.

Advantages

- It is fairly easy to start.
- Legal assistance is not a necessity.
- The organizational structure is simple.
- The owner has freedom to make decisions and enjoy the profits.
- It is easy to dissolve.

Disadvantages

- The owner is liable for all the enterprise's debts.

- Liability is not limited to the amount of capital/total assets invested in the business. The owner's home, car, bank account and other possessions may be claimed by people to whom he or she owes money.

- If the owner has personal debts, creditors can take assets of the business to satisfy demands.

- Sometimes it is difficult to obtain funding.

- Success is dependent on the owner's abilities.

- The legal life of the business terminates with the death of the owner.

Partnership

A **partnership** is the joining of two or more individuals to form an organization.

Advantages

- Gives you the opportunity to pool financial resources together.

- Provides the advantages of combining the additional skills and knowledge of partners. Allows the teaming of individuals who have complementary talent.

- Allows for division of labor and management responsibility.

Disadvantages

- General partners have unlimited liability.

- The death of a partner terminates the partnership.

- General partners are responsible for the acts of each other partner.

- Partners cannot obtain bonding protection against the acts of other partners.
- There is the possibility of disagreement among partners.

There are two different types of partnerships:

1) **General** - Each partner is held liable for the acts of other partners.

2) **Limited** - This form can only be created by compliance with a state's statutory requirements. It is composed of one or more general partners. The liability of the limited partner is limited to the amount he or she contributes.

A partnership should have an attorney draw up a partnership agreement. The partnership agreement usually includes sections addressing the following:

- name, purpose, and location
- duration of agreement
- type of partnership
- contribution by partners
- business expansion (how it will be handled)
- authority
- books, records, and the method of accounting
- division of profits and losses
- salaries
- rights of continuing partnership
- death of partner
- employee negotiations
- release of debts

- sale of partnership interests
- arbitration
- addition, alterations and/or modification of partnership agreement
- settlement of disputes
- required and prohibited acts
- absence and disability

Corporation

A **corporation** is a legal entity which is separate and distinct from the individual. In the new or very small corporation, the stock in the corporation is described as "closed" or "closely held" and is not available to the general public in order for the owners to keep control.

Advantages

- The corporate form of ownership offers permanence-the business does not cease to exist if an owner dies.

- Owners of a corporation have limited liability.

- Corporations usually have greater borrowing power.

- Transferring ownership is relatively easy.

- The corporate federal income tax rates are below the tax brackets for individuals

- Company expansion is relatively easy.

- In figuring the corporation's net income, salaries paid to employees and executives may be deducted as an expense item.

Disadvantages

- Incorporations can be costly and require detailed records which are often costly and time consuming.

- Corporate income is taxed twice. First, the corporation pays tax on its income before it distributes dividends, and then shareholders pay taxes on dividends.

- The powers of the corporation are limited to those stated in the charter.

- The corporate form of ownership is more impersonal than the other forms.

S Corporations

The **S Corporation**, formerly known as the Subchapter S Corporation, is a form of organization which is specifically designed for closely held firms. The major difference between this type of corporation and regular corporations is the way in which they are taxed. In S Corporations, the profits are distributed to shareholders according to how much stock they own. The shareholders pay tax on the profits as personal income with the corporation paying no tax as an entity. In essence, the stockholders are taxed as partners, thus avoiding the corporate income tax structure while allowing the firm to retain the limited liability feature of corporations.

S Corporations have many legal restrictions, including limitations to the number of stockholders, who may be stockholders, how profits are distributed and the amount of fringe benefits allowed owner/employees.

You should consult your attorney and accountant to determine the advantages and disadvantages of this and other forms of ownership for your particular business. You should also consult your accountant about all tax considerations prior to actually implementing your business.

Limited Liability Company

The **Limited Liability Company (LLC)** is a hybrid between a partnership and a corporation in that it combines the "pass-through" treatment of a partnership with the limited liability accorded to corporate shareholders.

Advantages

- Historically, most states require that a Limited Liability Corporation (LLC) be comprised of at least two LLC members. Today, most states and the IRS recognize the single-member LLC as a legitimate business structure.

- Like limited partnerships and corporations, the Limited Liability Corporation shares a similar advantage--it is recognized as a separate legal entity from its "members."

- Most states require fewer formalities be observed in an LLC in comparison to a corporation.

- The LLC owner's liability is generally limited to the amount of money which the person has invested in the LLC. Thus, LLC members are offered the same limited liability protection as a corporation's shareholders.

- LLCs allow for pass-through taxation. This means that earnings of an LLC are taxed only once. The earnings of an LLC are treated like the earnings from a partnership, sole proprietorships and most S corporations.

- Like general partnerships, LLCs are generally free to establish any organizational structure agreed on by the members. Thus, profit interests may be separated from voting interests.

Disadvantages

- Some states require that a LLC have more than one member

- Legal assistance is required to set up

- More paperwork is necessary than for an ordinary partnership

- Some states require that a dissolution date be listed in the articles of organization. This date may be amended. Further, certain events, such as death of a member, a member leaving, bankruptcy, etc. can be a dissolution event. A corporation has unlimited life and these events are not dissolution events for a corporation.

- The LLC is a newer entity, and people are not as familiar with the LLC as a corporation.

The major legal considerations for a small business are as follows:

I. Choice of organizational form of ownership

    A. Proprietorship
    B. Partnership - (general or limited)
    C. Corporation

II. Issues to address in organizational documents
    A. Procedures for voting
    B. Admission of new parties
    C. Providing continuity
    D. Resolving deadlocks
    E. Continuity in the event of death, disability or bankruptcy of an owner
    F. Sources of capital

III. Business issues to consider in structuring a company

    A. Exposure to liability

        1. Product liability
        2. Environmental protection
        3. Errors and omissions

      4. Fraud allegations
      5. Worker compensation
      6. Defamation
      7. Trademark and copyright infringement

   B. Regulatory authorities

      1. Licenses and permits
      2. Securities regulation
      3. Consumer protection
      4. Labor relations
      5. Environmental protection

IV. Registration with taxing authorities

   A. Federal income taxes
   B. Federal employment taxes and withholding
   C. State employment taxes
   D. Federal excise taxes
   E. State sales and use taxes
   F. State franchise and excise taxes
   G. Miscellaneous state taxes
   H. Local general property tax

Franchising

Franchising is a form of licensing by which the owner of a product, service or process obtains distribution at the retail level through affiliated dealers. The owner of the product or service is called the **franchisor**. The affiliated dealer is known as the **franchisee**. Common franchises include McDonalds, Burger King and Kiddie Academy. However, franchises are not limited to the food industries. Franchising is an option with many benefits. The benefits, however, vary from company to company.

Benefits

1. Franchising provides a chance to open a business without previous experience.
2. Franchising often provides a chance to open a business with less capital.
3. Many franchises provide financial assistance.
4. Franchises generally have a consumer-accepted image.
5. Franchises offer consistent quality.
6. Franchising affords combined buying power, allowing for purchasing advantages.
7. Franchises offer basic training and continued assistance.
8. Franchises provide location analysis.
9. Franchising provides the financial capability to buy a choice location.
10. Franchising provides advantageous rental or leasing rates.
11. Franchisers assist in the development of well-designed facilities, fixtures and displays and provide supplies.
12. Franchisers offer managerial and records assistance.
13. Franchisers offer sales, advertising and marketing assistance.
14. Franchisers provide national publicity, promotion and recognition.
15. Franchising affords higher income potential.
16. Franchises have a lower rate of failure.
17. Franchises provide continual research and development.

Disadvantages

Some of the disadvantages of franchising would include:

1. The subjugation of personal identity.

2. The submission to significant standardization and control.

3. The franchisee does not have the option of selecting unique services to offer.

Pointers for Evaluating a Franchise Opportunity

Before going into any franchise arrangement, the opportunity needs to be evaluated thoroughly. The following steps should be used when evaluating an opportunity:

1. Check the opportunity out with the Better Business Bureau and Chamber of Commerce.

2. Determine when the business was established.

3. Determine what type of financing is provided.

4. Ask the owners for a sample contract and study it with the advice of legal counsel.

5. Determine if the company provides continual assistance.

6. Find out how many of the franchises are now operating and where they are located.

7. Determine what has been the failure rate for the franchises.

8. Investigate how profits are running.

9. Research the product's or service's quality.

10. Evaluate the contract to be sure it covers all aspects of the agreement.

11. Investigate what types of promotion will be provided.

Franchising Checklist

Before any franchise agreement is signed, determine whether enough information about the proposed relationship has been obtained to understand fully the implications of the agreement. The following checklist may be useful in making that determination.[18]

The Company

How long has the firm been in business?
Has it a reputation for honesty and fair dealing?
How does it rate with the Better Business Bureau?
Is the firm adequately financed so that it can carry out its stated plan of financial assistance and expansion?
Has the franchisor shown you any certified figures indicating exact net profits of one or more operating firms which you have checked personally?
How selective is it in choosing franchisees?
Has the franchisor investigated you carefully enough to assure itself that you can successfully operate one of its franchises?

The Product

What is the product's quality?
How well is it selling?
Have you conducted a study to determine whether the product or service which you propose to sell has a market in your territory at the prices you will have to charge?
Is the product priced competitively?
Is it packaged attractively?
How long has it been on the market?
Where else is it sold?
Will the product or service you are considering be in greater demand, about the same, or less demand five years from now?

The Sales Area

Is the territory well defined?
Is it large enough to offer good sales potential?

What are its growth possibilities?
Does the franchise give you exclusive territorial rights or can the franchisor sell a second or third franchise in your territory?
Is the franchisor connected in any way with any other franchise company offering similar merchandise or services?
If the answer is yes, what is your protection against this second franchisor organization?
What competition exists in your territory for the product or service you contemplate selling?
What is the territory's income level? Are there fluctuations in income?
Will the population in the territory increase, remain static, or decrease over the next five years?

The Contract

Does the contract cover all aspects of the agreement?
Does it benefit both parties?
Has your lawyer approved the franchise contract?
Does the franchise call upon you to take any steps which are, according to your lawyer, unwise or illegal in your state, county or city?
Can the contract be renewed, terminated or transferred?
Under what conditions will the franchise be lost?
What are the conditions for obtaining a license?
Under what circumstances and at what cost can you terminate the franchise contract?
If you sell your franchise, will you be compensated for your goodwill or will the goodwill you have built into the business be lost by you?
Is a certain size and type of operation specified?
Is there an additional fixed payment each year?
Is there a percent of gross sales payment?
Must a certain amount of merchandise be purchased?
Is there an annual sales quota?
Can the franchisee return merchandise for credit?
Can the franchisee engage in other business activities?
Does the franchiser provide continuing assistance?
Will the firm assist you in finding a good location?
Is there training for franchisees and key employees?
Are manuals, sales kits, and/or accounting systems supplied?
Does the franchisor handle lease arrangements?
Does he or she design the store layout and displays?
Does he or she select opening inventory?
Does he or she provide inventory control methods?

Does he or she provide market surveys?
Does he or she help finance equipment?
Does he or she make direct loans to qualified individuals?
Does he or she actively promote the product or service?
How and where is the product being advertised?
What advertising aid does the franchisor provide?
What is the franchisee's share of advertising costs?
Exactly what can the franchiser do for you that you cannot do for yourself?

Questions Pertaining to Ownership

Answer the following questions to assess some of the key aspects of deciding what form of business organization is best for your firm.

What legal structure would insure the greatest adaptability for the administration of your firm?

What are the possibilities of attracting additional capital?

What are the needs for and possibilities of attracting additional expertise?

Which legal structure would best serve your purpose? Why?

"Formula for perpetual ignorance: Think you know it all."

M.G.L.J.

CHAPTER VI

Taking Over An Established Business

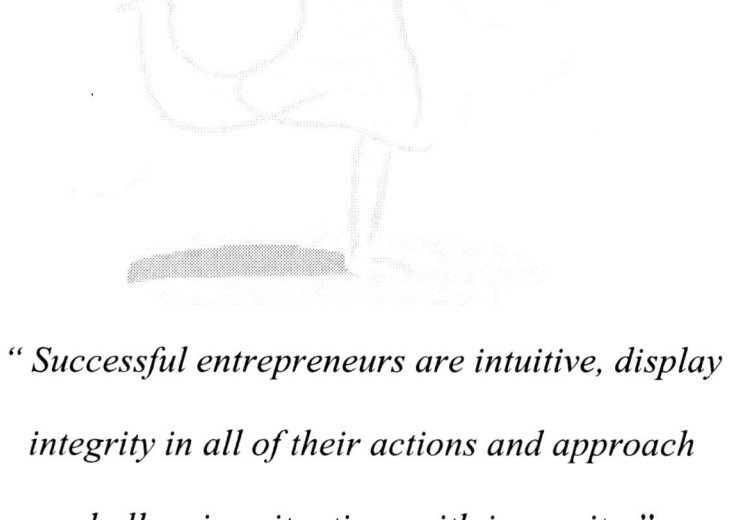

" Successful entrepreneurs are intuitive, display integrity in all of their actions and approach challenging situations with ingenuity."

M.G.L.J.

NEW BUSINESS VERSUS AN ESTABLISHED BUSINESS

The question may have already crossed your mind as to whether to buy a business that is already operating or to begin your own. Below are some considerations you should address when evaluating this question.

Just because a business is already established does not mean that success is guaranteed. The same very careful analysis that is conducted for a new enterprise must be done for an established business, including the consideration of target markets, location factors and capital requirements.

Acquiring an Established Business

Both pros and cons must be considered when the entrepreneur is making the decision about the feasibility of acquiring an existing enterprise.

The Pros

1. The building, equipment and people are already functioning.

2. The product is already being produced.

3. A market is established for the product or service.

4. Revenue is probably being generated.

5. The location may be desirable.

6. Financial relationships have been established.

7. Inventory is already in place.

8. Information about the business and industry can be obtained from the previous owner.

The Cons

1. The facilities may be old.

2. The personnel may be poor and inappropriate for the new owner.

3. Union/management relations may be bad.

4. The inventory, if any, may be out-of-date and useless.

5. The location may be poor.

6. The financial condition may be poor.

7. The firm's bad reputation may be inherited.

8. Space may be too expensive.

9. Equipment may be obsolete.

10. You may not know the real reason for the previous owner giving up the business.

11. Records may be misleading.

When taking over an established business, there are six factors which should be closely examined.

- The real reason for the business being terminated.

- The company's past sales and profits.

- The operating costs of the business (the use of operating ratios can be quite beneficial here).

- The condition of equipment and inventory (is it old, obsolete and/or in need of repair?).

- The value and condition of tangible assets.

- The value of the business as compared to the price being asked.

How to Enter an Existing Business

Examine the condition of the business by addressing the following:

1. Are the physical facilities run down?
2. Does the inventory contain mostly dead stock?
3. Is the market for the firm's product declining?
4. Is the business solvent?
5. What are the intentions of the present owner (health, retirement or competition)?

Business Evaluation Pointers

- Analyze accounting information, and do a physical inventory to determine the accuracy of recorded data.
- Determine whether the firm's cash position is high or low compared to the industry.
- Use financial ratios to determine the health of the firm. The following ratios are commonly used in the examination of the health of a firm.

Current Ratio: $\dfrac{\text{Current Assets}}{\text{Current Liabilities}}$

MEASURES SHORT-TERM SOLVENCY. SHOULD BE AROUND 2/1.

Quick Ratio: $\dfrac{\text{Current Assets - Inventory}}{\text{Current Liabilities}}$

SHOWS ABILITY TO PAY SHORT-TERM OBLIGATIONS WITHOUT HAVING TO SELL INVENTORY.

Debt to Equity Ratio: $\dfrac{\text{Current, Liabilities, and Bonds}}{\text{Equity}}$

SHOWS FIRM'S OBLIGATIONS TO CREDITORS

- Determine the amount of debt and the terms of that debt.

- Determine the validity of the financial statements.

- Check the age of the accounts receivable.

- Check the cash flow.

- Appraise the pricing formula.

- Appraise operations, plant and equipment.

- How effective are personnel?

- What is the quality of production?

- What is the physical condition of the plant? Is the layout appropriate for your needs?

- What is the age of the equipment?

- Conduct a feasibility study.

Establishing a New Business

So, why start a business from the ground up? Consider the pros and cons.

The Pros

1. You can create the physical facilities you want.

2. All modern equipment can be utilized as opposed to inheriting outdated equipment as may be the case when taking over an established business.

3. Modern processes and procedures can be implemented.

4. New inventory can be purchased.

5. New personnel can be hired.

6. You can design your own management system.

The Cons

1. There may be a problem selecting the right business to start.

2. The business has unproven performance records in sales, reliability, service and profits.

3. There are problems in finding a location, building, equipment and personnel.

4. The owner must train a new work force.

5. There is no established service quality.

6. There will be problems at the start.

7. There may be problems establishing an appropriate accounting system.

8. There will initially be "bugs" in the operations.

9. There may be problems establishing a customer or client base.

"Your reputation is your most valuable asset."

M.G.L.J.

CHAPTER VII

Location

"Be deliberate in your actions and move with determination and dignity."

M.G.L.J.

LOCATION

The importance of a good location should not be overlooked. Frequently a prospective entrepreneur in search of a business home will take a location simply because a vacancy exists. Many factors need to be considered when examining a possible location.

Reaching Potential Customers

An overall assessment should be made of the city or town in which one wishes to locate to determine its receptiveness to her or his type of business. More specifically, one should examine the territory where he or she expects to find customers and determine if the specific site will serve the needs of the potential customers. The following questions should be considered:

1. Do the identified potential customers have the money to afford the services you will be offering?

2. What are the neighborhood service-use patterns?

3. Is transportation convenient to the business?

4. What are the traffic patterns and volume near the proposed business location?

5. Is there a good primary and secondary road access to the business?

6. Are there plans for new road construction or alteration of the present roads which may involve the disruption of traffic near the business and/or a by-pass of the area?

7. Is there a good pool of qualified personnel available in the area?

Consider the enterprise location's proximity to major employers, public transportation, traffic arteries, etc. Other considerations are air quality and other environmental factors that impact outdoor activities (e.g., traffic, noise and volume, street safety, etc.).

Another factor to consider in site location is the location of competition. It is necessary to investigate the number of similar establishments competing for the same target market. Parking is a matter also deserving consideration. Ample parking is crucial in any business whose customers visit the business via car.

Of course, selecting a suitable building is also necessary, but this goes without saying and rests on good judgment as to the appropriateness of the facilities for the needs of the business.

LOCATION CONSIDERATIONS

Grade each factor: "E" for excellent, "G" for good, "F" for fair, and "P" for poor.

Factor	*Grade*
Centrally located to reach your target market	
Supplies and equipment readily available	
Nearby competition situation	
Transportation availability and rates	
Quantity and quality of available employees	
Prevailing rates of employee pay	
Parking facilities	
Adequacy of utilities (sewer, water, power, gas)	
Traffic flow	
Taxation burden	
Crime/Safety factors	
Quality of police and fire protection	
Physical suitability of building	
Type and cost of lease or mortgage	
Provision for future expansion	
Other businesses promoting area	
Image of area as it relates to business image	
Zoning restrictions	

"You can always tell the pioneers by the number of arrows in their back."

M.G.L.J.

CHAPTER VIII

Staffing

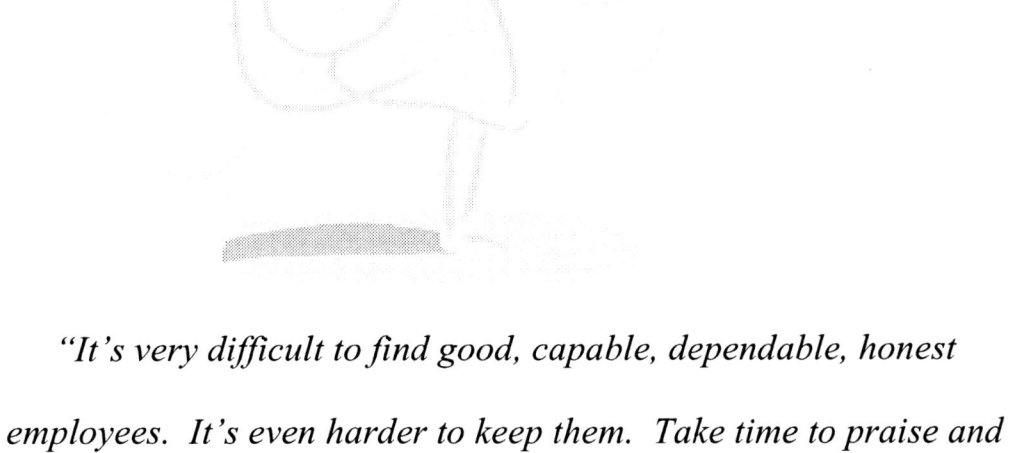

"It's very difficult to find good, capable, dependable, honest employees. It's even harder to keep them. Take time to praise and cherish your most valuable resources."

M.G.L.J.

STAFFING

Good, dependable employees are crucial for business success. Hence, careful attention needs to be placed on acquiring appropriate, qualified and reliable personnel. Policies must be developed for every aspect of your business, and personnel is no exception. You can determine your policies once you are in tune with your personality, your likes and dislikes, the objective and nature of your business and situations that might arise. You also need to consider the different matters which might arise affecting employees and how you wish to handle them. Such policies are considered in the scope of the personnel function, which is wide and varied. It encompasses planning, selection and assignment of employees, performance appraisal, training, development, wage and salary administration, employee benefits, employee services, employee relations, communications, work environment concerns, union relations, reports and record keeping, and equal employment/affirmative action.

When examining specific employee needs, you will need to determine what jobs are really necessary to accomplish your objectives and then look at the specifics of the job to determine what type of qualifications a person should have for that position. After determining your specific personnel needs, there are different sources from which you can obtain employees, such as the state employment service, private personnel agencies, newspaper ads, and local schools and colleges. Touching base with organizations, associations and people in the community, as well as displaying a sign in your window are all additional sources from which to obtain employees.

After deciding on the source or sources from which to obtain applicants, some form of screening process needs to be used so that the most appropriate person, based on the needs and desires of the firm, can be selected. It is necessary to develop a good application form in order to obtain all desired information, but make sure that questions are worded clearly and are in accordance with legal constraints (see next page for sample). References from applicants should also be requested. Applicants should, of course, be interviewed to find out as much as possible about the individual. The interview should involve asking specific, well thought-out questions, the answers to which should give enough information about the interviewee to make the decision to hire or not to hire him or her. All applicants being considered for the job should be thoroughly evaluated in terms of the job interview and references before making the hiring decision. Remember, hiring the wrong employee can be very costly and even disastrous, so take time with the hiring process.

APPLICATION FOR EMPLOYMENT

Applicant's Name (Last)	First	Middle Initial	Social Security Number - -
Mailing Address (Number)	Street		Work Telephone Number ( )
City State Zip Code e-mail			Home Telephone Number ( )

EDUCATION

Name of School	Location of School	Degree or Course of Study	Date Completed

Please indicate any special abilities, skills, training or relevant certifications that you feel particularly qualify you for the position.

EMPLOYMENT HISTORY – Begin with your most recent job. List each job separately.

Job Title	Dates Worked From _____ To _____	Pay $ _____ Per _____
Name of Employer	*Name of Supervisor*	
Address: City State Zip Code		
Telephone Number ( )	Reason for Leaving:	
Duties Performed:		
Job Title	Dates Worked From _____ To _____	Pay $ _____ Per _____
Name of Employer	*Name of Supervisor*	
Address: City State Zip Code		
Telephone Number ( )	Reason for Leaving:	
Duties Performed:		
Job Title	Dates Worked From _____ To _____	Pay $ _____ Per _____
Name of Employer	*Name of Supervisor*	
Address: City State Zip Code		
Telephone Number ( )	Reason for Leaving:	
Duties Performed:		

May we contact the employers previously listed?   If not, indicate which ones you do not wish us to contact.

PERSONAL REFERENCES: List the names of three references that we may contact.

1) Name	Telephone # ( )	Relationship (Teacher etc.)
Address: City State Zip Code		
2) Name	Telephone # ( )	Relationship (Teacher etc.)
Address: City State Zip Code		
3) Name	Telephone # ( )	Relationship (Teacher etc.)
Address: City State Zip Code		

Training

The training aspect of personnel is an area often neglected in terms of importance. The success of a business rests heavily on having qualified, well-trained employees. The nature of training can take a variety of formats, such as on-the-job training, apprenticeships, internships, outside training, vestibule training, classroom training and a myriad of combinations. Some outside training programs which may be of interest to the entrepreneur include the following:

- Manpower Development Training Act of 1962: Provides federal assistance in training unemployed and underemployed workers. The government reimburses you for part of the wages and training.

- Economic Opportunity Act (Anti-Poverty) of 1964: Firms hire individuals, and the
- government pays the cost of training.

- The JOBS Program (Job Opportunities in the Business Sector):

- You submit a proposal for contracts to provide on-the-job training for the disadvantaged employed and you are paid additional costs incurred because of limited qualifications of those hired and trained.

- Training Programs offered by personnel development firms.

Considerations in Setting Pay

Employers must address the issue of the level of compensation for their employees. Factors generally considered are:

- Effort and time required for the job
- The entrepreneur's ability to pay

- Cost of living
- Government regulation
- Labor union considerations
- Supply and demand for workers, education level of employees and industry and area rates
- Incentive plans
- Bonuses based on profit
- Pension plans

Employee Relations

The following guidelines can be used in handling employee grievances effectively:

1. Assure employees that complaining will not prejudice their relationship with their immediate superior.

2. Provide a clear way of presenting grievances.

3. Minimize red tape and time in processing grievances.

4. Provide a way for employees who cannot express themselves easily to present grievances.

All employees should receive a handbook containing major company policies and employee concern areas.

EMPLOYEE HANDBOOK

SAMPLE TABLE OF CONTENTS

I. WELCOME MESSAGE

II. HISTORY OF THE COMPANY

III. THIS IS OUR BUSINESS

IV. YOU AND YOUR FUTURE

V. WHAT YOU WILL NEED TO KNOW

    Working Hours
    Reporting to Work
    "Time Clock"
    Rest Periods
    Absence from Work
    Reporting Absences
    Employment Record
    Pay Period
    Shift Premiums
    Safety and Accident Prevention
    Use of Telephones
    How to Make Complaints

VI. THESE ARE YOUR BENEFITS
    Vacations
    Holidays
    Group Insurance
    Hospitalization and Surgical Benefits
    Free Parking
    Christmas Bonus
    Savings Plan
    Profit-Sharing Plan
    Suggestion Award
    Jury Duty
    Military Leave
    U. S. Old Age Benefits

VII. THESE SPECIAL SERVICES ARE FOR YOU
    Credit Union
    Education Plans
    Medical Dispensary
    Bowling League

VIII. PERTINENT BUSINESS POLICIES

IX. INDEX

A potential investor, as well as the originator of a business venture, will need to know the key personnel who will be carrying out the objectives of the business. It is necessary for the entrepreneur to pull together a dynamic management and work team who possess the appropriate and necessary skills and knowledge to make the business a success. A good business plan encompasses the resumes of all of the key individuals in charge of operating the business. On the following page you will find a suggested format for including information about all key personnel. Make sure that you capitalize on all skills, experience and training that directly and indirectly relate to the nature of the proposed venture. Make sure that you have aligned yourself with the right combination of key persons. At this time, you may want to go back to Chapter I and reassess your skills, abilities and personal characteristics. Make sure that you have personnel who can compensate for your weak areas and strengthen your stronger areas.

Sample Resume Format
For
Business Principals

                                                  Address   Phone, Fax, E-mail

Name

Experience — (List your current or most recent job first; positions held and name of companies; work experience and knowledge in the field of the proposed venture)

Education — (Begin with highest level attained, including schools and year graduated or year training was completed; major and minor courses of study; significant school activities.) Be certain to highlight training relevant to your proposed venture.

Special Skills and/or Certifications — (List all specialized training, skills and relevant certifications)

Professional Affiliations — (List all professional organizations in which you hold membership)

Community and Civic Affiliations — (List all community involvement and volunteer service activities)

References — (List at least 3 good references, preferably individuals well known in the industry of your proposed business venture or well known in the community, nationally or locally.)

ENTREPRENEURS

1. What key managerial skills and expertise does the proposed venture need to succeed?

2. Indicate the crucial skills necessary for success (attorneys, marketing people, accountants)

3. Indicate the primary individuals involved in your firm including co-founders and their principal skills. Include your own skills and experience with this type of business.

4. List the type of personnel needed for the operation of your business. Include an employee handbook in this section along with responsibilities of all personnel. (See example of Table of Contents.) All firms, regardless of size, should prepare an employee handbook which summarizes employee concern areas and policies and serves as an easy reference for the employee as well as the employer.

"When we are foolish we want to conquer the world.

When we are wise we want to conquer ourselves."

M.G.L.J.

CHAPTER IX

Organizing Your Business

Details, Details, Details.

"Pay attention to the details even though it may seem that you are spending too much time on them.

Excellence is in the details."

M.G.L.J.

ORGANIZING YOUR BUSINESS

Regardless of the size of your business venture, there is a need for some systematic way of doing things or some form of organization. A good way of approaching organizational structure is to consider all the activities necessary to accomplish the objectives of the firm. Categorize or put these activities into feasible groupings, and establish appropriate authority for each grouping. The entrepreneur must thoroughly define the personnel required for the accomplishment of the activities of each grouping, prepare an organizational chart and then thoroughly re-examine all activities and groupings for efficiency and effectiveness.

Such a procedure involves delegation of authority and responsibility. Delegation itself is often difficult for the entrepreneur because it involves letting loose of some of the decision making and some control. But proper delegation of authority is necessary for success. One of the main keys to effective delegation is knowing what to delegate and having competent and reliable employees to whom to delegate. With the delegation of authority goes the assignment of responsibility for the completion of the delegated tasks. However, accountability cannot be delegated. The entrepreneur is responsible for the successful operation of the firm, and how successfully the delegated tasks are accomplished will still fall back on the business owner's shoulders. So the importance of competent employees is evident along with the necessity for a formalized system of control.

Basic Organizing Principles

1. Unity of Command

Employees should have only one superior to whom they are directly responsible.

2. Parity of Authority

Authority should be equal with responsibility. When delegating responsibility, measures must be taken to make sure employees have enough authority to carry out their duties and responsibilities, but not more authority than necessary. Make sure employees have a written statement of their duties, authority, responsibilities, and relationships.

Ways of Organizing Your Business

Seven common ways of structuring a business include organizing by the following:

1. **Function** - similar skills are grouped to form a functional unit

2. **Product** - the business is structured according to the individual services offered to the public.

3. **Process** - similar processes, such as teaching or food services for children, are the basis for organizing the firm.

4. **Geographic area** - some firms have locations in different geographical areas and are organized primarily on the basis of territorial concerns.

5. **Type of customers serviced** - some firms service different types of customers, such as infants and pre-schoolers and are structured accordingly.

6. **Project** - some firms, such as consulting businesses, are organized internally based on projects being researched or worked on.

7. **Individual talents of subordinates** - some organizations are structured based on the particular areas of expertise of employees.

Following, you will find a simple organizational chart for a small child care. This organizational structure shows an obvious direct relationship between the owner and the children served. With growth comes the need for a slightly more complex structure and the delegation of duties. The second chart illustrates growth in this firm. As the firm continues to grow, it will become necessary to bring in more personnel and divide up more of the duties and responsibilities by creating new positions and/or departments.

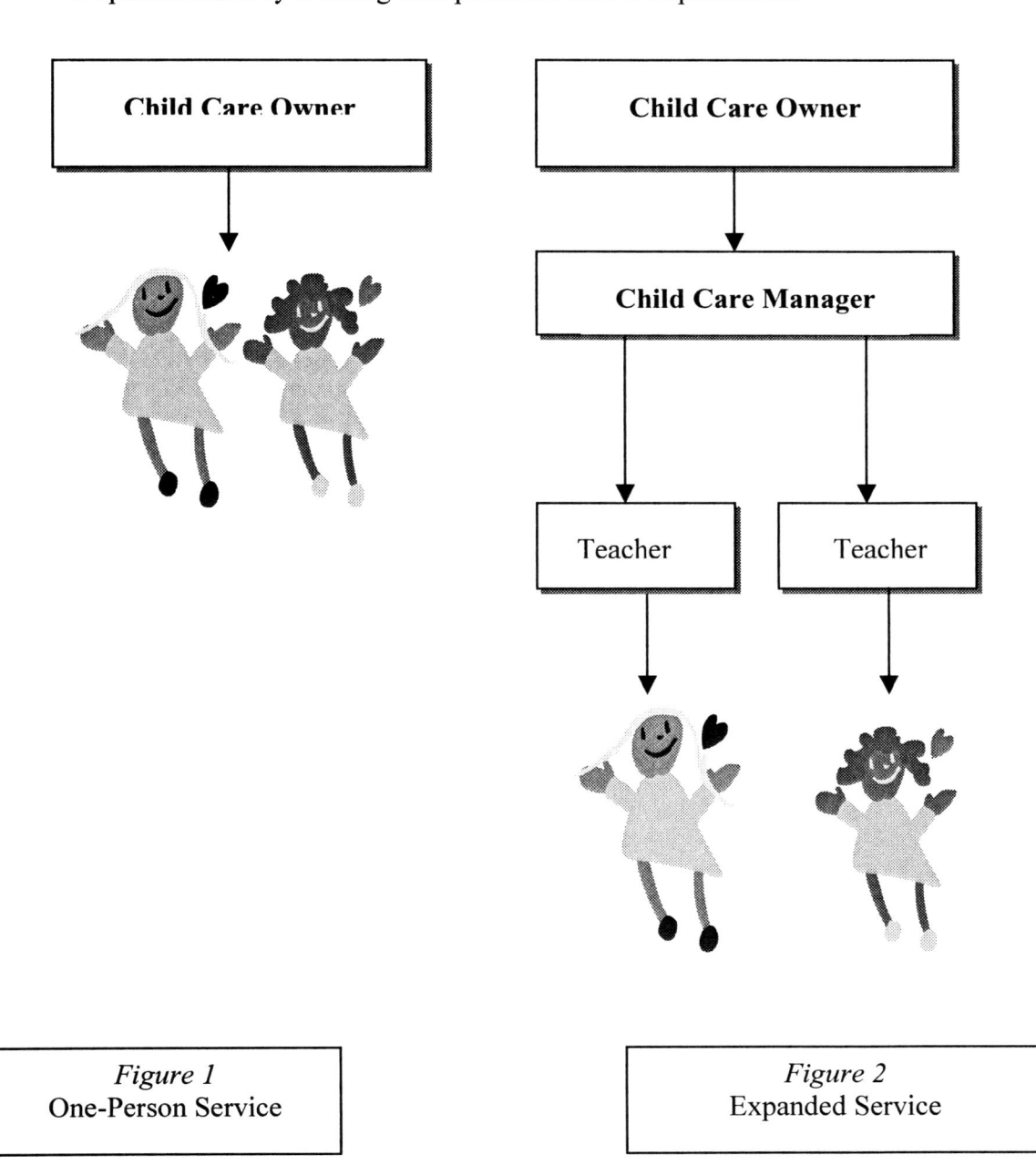

Figure 1
One-Person Service

Figure 2
Expanded Service

"Never avoid the numbers. They are the thermometer indicating and health and wealth of your business."

M.G.L.J.

CHAPTER X

Financing Your Business

"It's not all about dollars and cents. Teaching a child is an investment in the future of our country that can reap higher dividends than any financial investment known to humanity."

M.G.L.J.

FINANCING YOUR BUSINESS

If you are on a limited budget, a good initial strategy is to minimize your outlay on physical items and spend more on equipment, advertising and your services. All businesses, regardless of the type, will need money to get started and to operate.

After you determine the size of your initial operations, you will have to follow an estimating process of the costs of these items and any others appropriate for your establishment. You will need to have enough cash to take care of your operational expenses for several months. Your capital, in essence, should provide enough to keep you going until you can start turning a profit.

The capital you need to be acquiring is often grouped into several categories:

1. Fixed capital: money for the building, equipment, fixtures and vehicles.

2. Working capital: money for running the business on a day-to-day basis. This covers items such as utilities, money for buying inventory, insurance, advertising, salaries, rent, savings, cash, accounts receivable, etc.

3. Funds for personal living costs: capital to provide for you and your family until the business brings a profit.

4. Money cushion: extra money for unforeseen and unexpected costs.

It is crucial to have sufficient capital. The drawbacks of not having enough capital include:

- business failure
- inability to afford good employees

- investment in sub-standard or inadequate equipment
- inadequate inventory
- inability to obtain a good credit rating
- inability to obtain quantity discounts and other cost advantages

After thoroughly assessing your monetary requirements for starting and operating your venture, you will need to identify sources from which monies can be obtained for starting and operating your venture. There are many ways to obtain money to start and operate your business. Business financing is categorized as either **equity** or **debt financing**.

Equity financing represents money which the owner and/or others put into the business. All parties are at risk and at the same time stand to reap rewards. Equity financing is used for starting a business, expanding a business and financing acquisitions. Equity financing includes personal savings and assets, money from family and friends, investments by key employees and funds from venture capitalists.

Debt financing, on the other hand, is money loaned to businesses for a fee or interest. The funds borrowed, therefore, must be repaid. Debt financing is also used for business start up, operating funds and expansion funds. Debt financing includes funds from commercial banks, savings and loans, savings bonds, commercial finance companies, small business investment corporations, federal programs, franchisers or project organizers.

There are many sources from which funds may be borrowed. They include the following:

Private investors: Members of the family, friends, business associates, equipment dealers (if the equipment is bought on an installment basis or leased) and wholesalers of products (when they offer 30 to 90 days of credit before demanding payment).

Business firms: Various business sources, such as:

- Banks

- Savings and loan companies which refinance home mortgages and make property improvement loans

- Personal finance companies

- Finance companies which provide commercial credit (listed in the yellow pages and advertised in classified and financial sections of newspapers)

- Life insurance companies (some make loans to policy holders)

- Small business investment companies (these companies are licensed by the Small Business Administration to make long-term loans and guarantee bank loans and they will provide equity financing by actually buying a share of the business)

- Development corporations which are formed by private citizens or businesses to promote the economy in their area

- Venture capital associations or groups of investors looking for businesses with promising futures (they usually provide equity financing, and they often advertise in the classified section of the newspaper Want Ads and via various website listings)

Federal Government: Some of the federal funding sources available are:

- Small Business Administration (SBA)//
- Veterans Administration (VA)

Commercial Banks: One of the major sources of borrowing capital is a local commercial bank. It is crucial to have good rapport with your banker. Loans are generally either short-term or long-term in nature. Short-term generally represents money extended for a year or less, and long-term represents money extended for a period over a year. Loans are categorized as secured/collateral loans or unsecured. In the first type, the borrower is asked to pledge something such as life insurance, securities, equipment, real estate or some other asset belonging to the loan seeker or the business. In the second instance, no security is required and the loan is made based more on one's financial reputation, managerial ability, bank's evaluation of the business's soundness, etc. Your personal character, business reputation, adequate records, ability to repay the loan and suitable collateral are all important necessities in obtaining a loan.

Personal Savings, Family and Friends: Your personal savings should be used as a last resort. If you obtain a loan from a bank, always spend the bank's money first.

Friends and family will frequently be receptive to lending you money, particularly if your business plan reflects significant research, and you can convince them that you can give them a greater return on their money than they would be able to obtain from a bank. Be sure when using this form of financing that you protect yourself with a buy-back contract or promissory note at the beginning of the financial relationship. The contract should make it worthwhile for your friends and family to invest in your business. At the same time, it should protect your ownership in the company when you become highly successful. Be cautious with family and friends' financial assistance. Personal relationships can become extremely strained when money is involved.

Life Insurance Policies: Individuals can borrow a major percentage of the cash value of their life insurance policies that have "paid-in" equity. These loan rates are generally much lower than bank loan rates. This form of financing should be investigated if you have such policies, but make sure you know any and all ramifications of borrowing on the equity.

Credit Cards: Credit cards are the most expensive way to finance your business due to the comparatively high interest rates. Try to avoid this form of financing.

Suppliers: Be familiar with all trade credit options. Creative terms with vendors can significantly affect your cash flow so that you have more money available when it is needed. Also, many suppliers, just for the asking, will pay you money if you are using their products. For example, a manufacturer or distributor of play gyms may compensate you if you advertise that you are only using their specially constructed and safe equipment.

Mortgaging Real Estate: Mortgages on residential property may sometimes be used to finance a business. You should contact your mortgage company for specific information about this form of financing. Be sure to assess the ramifications of using this form of financing, including the fact that you may lose your property if the loan is not repaid in a timely manner.

Savings and Loan Associations: Savings and loan associations historically have specialized in real estate financing, making loans on commercial, industrial and residential properties. Savings and loan associations are now also beginning to offer the usual type of business loans available through commercial banks.

Venture Capitalists: Venture capitalists are affluent investors who need tax write-offs. They will invest money in your firm in return for your making them limited partners in your business. The majority of all new businesses have losses at first, and some wealthy investors are looking for losses to get tax breaks. You should obtain the assistance of an accountant and attorney before getting involved with venture capitalists.

Small Business Administration: The SBA defines a small business as one that is independently owned and operated and not dominant in its field. They have the specific objective of promoting the small business contribution to the nation's economic growth. By law, they are not allowed to make a loan if the funds can be obtained from a bank or other private source. Therefore, the first step is to try to obtain financing through regular channels. If the loan is turned down, then ask the bank to make the loan under SBA's Loan Guaranty Plan or participate with SBA in a loan. If the banker is interested, ask her or him to contact the SBA to discuss your application. Usually the SBA will deal directly with the banker. The Small Business Administration will consider making a direct loan when these other forms of financing are not obtainable.

Summary of types of loans available from SBA:

1. Guarantee Loan: The SBA will guarantee up to a certain amount of money loaned to a small businessperson.

2. Participation Loan: SBA and the lending institution each put up part of the funds for the loan.

3. Economic Opportunity Loan: The SBA will lend money to any resident of the United States, Puerto Rico or Guam if:

    a. Total family income from all sources (excluding welfare) is not sufficient for the basic needs of the family, and

    b. Due to social or economic disadvantages, the person has been denied the opportunity to acquire adequate financing through normal channels or reasonable terms. This include honorably discharged Vietnam-era veterans.

4. Lease Guarantee Program: This is the issuance of an insurance policy or the reinsuring of a policy issued by a private insurance company which guarantees the rent for a small businessperson. A small business is often unable to lease a strategic location because it does not have a prime credit rating as required by some property owners. A guarantee that the rent will not be defaulted on is a valuable negotiating tool in locating a site.

5. Minority Loans: Loans are processed under somewhat relaxed criteria to encourage minority individuals to pursue business ownership.

The SBA also furnishes individual assistance to small businesspersons in the form of counseling, advice and specific information of various types of business enterprises. The SBA requires all information and an assortment of papers that any other lender would. They will ask the same questions. They require collateral or some other guarantee of repayment, though good character and business ability may weigh more heavily with them than with a bank. However, they do state that the borrower should be able to provide sufficient funds from his or her own resources to have a reasonable amount at stake in the early stages of a new business. Certain SBA loan programs are phased in and others eliminated periodically, so check with your local SBA office for additional information.

Veterans Administration: The purpose of the VA program is to enable the veteran to obtain home, farm or business real estate, supplies and equipment, and working capital. The VA guarantees or insures various types of loans made by private lenders. If you qualify, then the various lenders (banks, savings and loans, etc.) would have to be contacted to determine if they make VA business loans and to set up an appointment. If a loan is not available in this way, the VA can make a direct loan in some cases.

Additional Ways of Obtaining Financing: Various other types of financing are as follows:

1. Financing by selling ownership of the business: Partnership arrangements, corporate arrangements and public venture capitalists or small business investment companies (SBIC's) which are privately owned venture capital firms eligible for federal loans to invest in or loan to businesses.

2. Commercial Finance Companies: Firms which specialize in higher risk loans and generally charge higher interest rates than commercial banks.

3. Consumer Finance Companies: Financing arranged as a personal loan to one or several of the people in the business.

4. Trade Credit: Obtaining credit and financing from suppliers by their extension of terms of payment.

5. Factoring: This form of financing involves the outright sale of a business' accounts receivables to another firm, called a factor. The factor then pays cash to the business for its accounts receivables at a charge for each invoice plus interest on its advance.

Pointers for Successful Debt Financing

- If you are presently working, try to borrow funds while still employed. Studies show that banks are less likely to give you a loan when you do not have a "steady job.

- Make sure that you have devoted great attention to your marketing plan. Bankers want to know that there is actually a substantial market for your business and that you know how to capture the market successfully.

- Be able to sell yourself to the banker, and this includes looking like a businessperson.

- Try to search out a banker who is familiar with your industry.

- Fill out loan documents and applications neatly and accurately.

- Keep trade secrets to yourself. Do not share the details of your unique features unnecessarily. Share enough to establish the fact that you can obtain the competitive edge in the market, but the banker does not need to know everything.
- Under capitalization is a major cause of business failure. Make sure you have accurately assessed your start-up and working capital requirements for at least one year before you initiate your venture. Examine all of the financing sources mentioned in this chapter and determine what is right for you. A sample personal financial statement is included in the appendix to help you determine your personal net worth and assess what collateral you may have to assist you in finding funding for your venture.

CHAPTER XI

Business Records

"Tough times don't last, but tough women do."

M.G.L.J.

BUSINESS RECORDS

The novice entrepreneur probably would want to use the services of an accountant to set up the appropriate business accounting records. The following information is designed to provide you with some insight as to the types of records your accountant should establish, the purpose of each of these records, and the information they should provide you.

Before obtaining funds from whichever source is feasible, it is necessary to have accurate financial records and statements to present to your potential funder. These records are also necessary for successful business operations. Keeping accurate, concise and appropriate business records is necessary for business success. A great majority of businesses that have failed did not keep accurate records. Good records show whether a business is making a profit, how much profit, and whether the business is efficient and growing. Good records also help you to identify specific problem areas.

For the purpose of efficient business operations as well as funding attainment, all businesses need the following basic financial records:

- **A Record of Cash and Record of Sales Receipts**
- **The Balance Sheet** lists the firm's assets and liabilities. It shows what the business is worth, what the owner owes, and what its obligations are. To be accurate, total assets must equal total liabilities plus owner's equity.
- **The Profit/Loss Statement**, which is often called the Income Statement, lists the total sales, cost of goods sold or services rendered, expenses and taxes required in order to obtain a profit, usually for a period of a month. It

may take different forms, but is generally a statement of the total amount of goods or services sold less all expenses and costs levied against sales to determine profit or loss from one's operations. Again, this is another statement which helps the entrepreneur determine the efficiency of the business operations and locate problem areas, and it addresses the question of whether or not a profit was made. The most common method of measuring profit is to find out what net profit is, and this is usually calculated on a monthly basis. This is found by taking the total sales for the month and subtracting the cost of sales which is the total of all expenditures that went directly into whatever was sold.

- **Accounts Payable Record** represents a list of one's suppliers and the amount owed to each.

- **Accounts Receivable Record** shows a list of what each credit customer owes you. It should also show what and when each customer purchases, and is a record of all payments received.

- **Cash Payments Journal** shows all expenditures, including date, expense identity, and reason,

- **Payroll Record** shows gross and net amounts of salaries paid, date of transactions, amount of taxes withheld and holdings.

- **Schedule of Depreciation** calculates the decrease in value of equipment and furnishings so as to determine net worth. Depreciation schedules are basically lists of the major equipment and furnishings a company owns.
- **Withdrawal and Capital Record** shows what the owner puts in or takes out of the business and serves as a record of transactions which affect ownership.

Good records should show the financial status of the business, trends in the business, and provide important information about your business as well as point to problem areas. The following sample statements, presented in simplistic form, illustrate the usage of several basic records. The actual records and statements for an operating business, of course, will involve more detailed work than these three (3) statements, and again, it is recommended that the services of an experienced accountant be employed.

Happy Days Child Care Center
Income Statement
For Month Ended July 31, 20__

Service Fees		$ 30,000.00
Operating Expenses		
Salaries	$ 2,000.00	
Rent Expense	700.00	
Automobile Expense	400.00	
Supplies	100.00	
Insurance	500.00	
Miscellaneous Expenses	200.00	
Total Operating Expenses		3,900.00
Net Income		$26,100.00

This Income Statement shows the total sales for the month of July, which were $30,000.00, from which was subtracted the total expenses for that same period of $3,900.00, thereby providing the total net income for the month of July of $26,100.00.

Happy Days Child Care Center
Capital Statement
For Month Ended July 31, 20__

Capital, July 1, 20__		$10,000.00
Net Income for July	$26,100.00	
Less Withdrawals	2,000.00	
Increase in Capital		24,100.00
Capital, July 31, 20__		34,100.00

The Capital Statement shows the amount of capital the owner had in the business at the beginning of the time period, which was $10,000.00 on July 1. To this amount is added the net income for the month of July of $26,100.00 which can be determined by looking at your income statement, less withdrawals of $2,000.00 yielding an increase in capital of $24,100.00. The increase in capital for the month of July added to the beginning capital gives the total capital position at the end of the month of $34,100.00

Happy Days Child Care Center
Balance Sheet
July 31, 20__

Assets

Cash	$18,600.00
Accounts Receivable	15,000.00
Supplies	3,000.00
Total Assets	36,600.00

Liabilities

Accounts Payable	$ 2,500.00

Capital

M. Lawncom, Capital	$34,100.00
Total Liabilities & Capital	$36,600.00

The Balance Sheet visually depicts the accounting equation: Assets = Liabilities + Owner's Equity. This statement lists the firm's total assets as of July 31, which were $36,600.00, along with the total liabilities or total debt of the firm of $2,500.00, and the owner's capital of $34,100.00.

$$A = L + OE$$

$$\$36,600.00 = \$2,500.00 + \$34,100.00$$

A potential financier for a new business will be particularly interested in the following information and statements:

1. Start-Up Costs (Estimated)
2. Owner's Living Expenses (Estimated)
3. Operating Costs (Projected)
4. Balance Sheet (Projected)
5. Profit/Loss (Income) Statement (Projected)
6. Cash Flow Statement (Projected)
7. Break-Even Analysis

The small business owner on a daily basis should:

1. Check cash on hand.
2. Check the bank balance.
3. Check the daily summary of sales and cash receipts.
4. Make sure that all errors in recording collections on accounts are corrected.
5. Make sure that a record of all monies paid out, by cash or check, is maintained.

The small business owner on a weekly basis should:

1. Check accounts receivable, and take action on delinquent accounts.
2. Check accounts payable, and take advantage of discounts for early payment.
3. Make sure payroll records are in order.
4. Make sure taxes and reports to State and Federal Government are prepared and sent.

The small business owner on a monthly basis should:

1. Make sure that all Journal entries are posted to the General Ledger.

2. Assess the Profit/Loss Statement.

3. Assess the Balance Sheet.

4. Make sure the Bank Statement is reconciled.

5. Make sure the Petty Cash Account is in balance.

6. Make sure that all Federal Tax Deposits, Withheld Income and FICA Taxes (Form 501) and State Taxes are made.

7. Make sure that Accounts Receivable are aged, i.e., 30, 60, 90 days, etc., and collect past dues.

8. Check inventory.

"It's not the one who falls that fails, but the one who falls, gives up, and never gets up."

M.G.L.J.

CHAPTER XII

Sources of Supply and Inventory

"You will pass those who discouraged you from pursuing your entrepreneurial dreams on the stairway to success. They will be sitting on the steps, still passing out negative thoughts and going nowhere"

M.G.L.J.

SOURCES OF SUPPLY AND INVENTORY

Before it can be determined that a business is feasible, it is necessary to identify sources from which the entrepreneur may obtain goods either for use in the business or for resale.

Retail establishments generally deal with wholesalers or manufacturers for merchandise. This investigation is very important because the potential entrepreneur may find it difficult to locate suppliers willing to deal with them, particularly on a small volume basis. The entrepreneur may determine, based on the prices of goods purchased from the supply source and the necessary markup in light of overhead, that it will be too difficult to compete on a price basis with competitors. The **Thomas Register** is a good starting point for identifying potential suppliers. This register contains a listing of all supply sources arranged according to product. It is important that a business not be developed relying totally on one supplier. If the business encounters problems with this one supplier or the supplier is slow in the delivery of purchases, the entrepreneur's operations may be significantly affected. It is best to use several supply sources continuously so as to establish good credit and rapport with these firms. Resultantly, the entrepreneur will get better service once he or she is recognized as a consistent customer.

It is important to have an inventory control system set up which will indicate when you need to reorder certain items such as food items or educational supplies. Inventory records allow one to keep an accurate account of the amount and nature of inventory at any one point. Maintaining inventory records by hand can be a complicated and tedious chore, and some small firms have begun using electronic data processing (EDP) which can provide the entrepreneur with valuable information allowing time to make good purchasing decisions quickly.

CHAPTER XIII

Sales Forecasting

"Trying times are times for trying new ideas."

M.G.L.J.

SALES FORECASTING

Once the decision has been made to go into business and the type of business has been selected, the next step is to forecast sales of goods or services for at least the first year. This is not an easy task, as you are dealing with many unknown factors; nevertheless, it is necessary to attempt to make an intelligent forecast using sound rationale. Sales forecasting requires you to predict the future as accurately as possible with justification for the forecasted figures. A forecast can be based on your personal judgment, interviews with people operating similar businesses, various types of published data, information from experts, as well as market calculations. Factors to take into consideration when forecasting sales include industry trends for your area; forecasts for child care in your state, city and area; and an assessment of your competition.

One approach to developing a sales forecast begins by estimating the total number of persons in the selected target market. This estimate comes from an analysis of your market via a survey and also from secondary sources such as **Statistical Abstracts of the U. S.**, marketing and demographic informational sources, and industry publications.

The following four equations will allow you to forecast sales:

(1) T x A = TPM

(2) TPM x P = TAM

(3) TAM x EMS = Sales in Units

(4) Sales in Units x PR = Sales in Dollars

Explanation:

(1) T x A = TPM

Total number of people in the target market multiplied by the annual number of purchases per person = total potential market.

(2) TPM x P = TAM

Total potential market multiplied by the percent of the total market coverage you think you might be able to obtain = total available market.

(3) TAM x EMS = Sales in Units

Total available market multiplied by the expected market share you expect to obtain = sales forecast in units.

(4) Sales in Units x PR = Sales in Dollars

Sales forecast in units multiplied by the price per unit = sales forecast in dollars.

When determining your expected market share, be sure to take into consideration the present market share of your competitors, the amount of promotion you will be using compared to your competition, the sales trends of similar services and what the present competition may do to improve their present service when you enter the market.

CHAPTER XIV

The Investment Prospectus

"There is no escalator to success.   You have to take the stairs."

M.G.L.J.

THE INVESTMENT PROSPECTUS

All important information about your business can strategically and for, impact purposes, be summarized in an investment prospectus. Someone considering investing in your business or lending you money wants to know exactly and quickly how much money you need and why they should lend it to you. (How profitable is it going to be?) Profit is important to an investor; however, many individuals considering venture initiation get entwined in the development of their idea into a business and fail to look at how profitable it stands to be. An outline of an investment prospectus follows.

Investment Prospectus Outline

Cover letter describing:
    Nature of business
    Amount of financing needed
    Terms of loan

Business description:
    Name and location
    Nature of business
    Organizational structure
    Product or service description
    Business goals
    Summary of financial needs and proposed use of funds

Market strategy:
    Market analysis
    Target market
    Competition
    Marketing objectives
    Price policies
    Distribution system
    Promotion

Production:
    Suppliers
    Production methods

Product services
Patents, legal and technical information

Management:
Management/ownership structure
Education and work experience of board of directors and key personnel
Personnel plan
Compensation policy

Financial data:
Financial statements
Profit and loss statements (monthly for one year with explanation of projections)
Balance sheets (projected one year after loan or investment with explanation of projections)
Cash flow projection (monthly for one year with explanation of projections)
Specific uses of investment funds
Credit references

CHAPTER XV

Is It Feasible?

"If the word QUIT is part of your vocabulary, then the word FINISH is likely not."

Anonymous

IS IT FEASIBLE?

Your final considerations should address whether or not your proposed venture is feasible. Make sure you reiterate all significant justifications in this section.

The SBA provides a convenient checklist for those going into business. The following checklist affords a good opportunity to go back and make sure you have considered all necessary factors. Answer each question with a yes/no response. Then go back and evaluate your responses throughout the entire publication and determine if your considered business venture is feasible and has a significant chance for success.

YOU

Are you the kind of person who can get a business started and make it go?

____ Think about why you want to own your own business. Do you want a business badly enough to work long hours without knowing how much money you will end up with?

____ Have you worked in a business like the one you want to start?

____ Have you worked for someone else as a supervisor or manager?

____ Have you had any business training in school?

____ Have you saved any money?

MONEY

____ Do you know how much money you will need to get your business started?

____ Have you counted how much of your own money you can put into the business?

____ Do you know how much credit you can get from your suppliers--the people you will buy from?

____ Do you know where you can borrow the rest of the money you need to start your business?

____ Have you figured out what net income per year you can expect to get from the business? Count your salary and your profit on the money you put into the business.

____ Can you live on less than that amount so that you can use some of it to help your business grow?

____ Have you talked to a banker about your plans?

FORM OF BUSINESS

____ If you need a partner with money or know-how that you do not have, do you know someone appropriate and someone you can get along with?

____ Do you know the good and bad points about going into business alone, having a partner and incorporating your business?

____ Have you talked to a lawyer about the appropriate form of ownership?

CUSTOMERS OR CLIENTS

____ Do most businesses in your community seem to be doing well?

____ Have you tried to find out whether enterprises like the one you want to open are doing well in your community and in the rest of the country?

____ Do you know what kind of people will want to buy what you plan to sell?

____ Do people such as that live in the area where you want to open your business?

____ Do they need a business like yours?

____ If not, have you thought about opening a different kind of enterprise or going to another neighborhood?

YOUR BUILDING

____ Have you found a good building for your business?

____ Will you have enough room when your business gets bigger?

____ Can you fix the building the way you want it without spending too much money?

____ Can people get to it easily from parking spaces, bus stops or their homes?

____ Have you had a lawyer check the lease and zoning restrictions?

EQUIPMENT AND SUPPLIES

____ Do you know just what equipment and supplies you need and how much they will cost?

YOUR SERVICE

____ Have you decided what services you will sell?

____ Do you know how much or how many of each you will buy to open your business?

____ Have you found suppliers who will sell you what you need at a good price?

____ Have you compared the prices and credit terms of different suppliers?

YOUR RECORDS

____ Have you planned a system of records that will keep track of your income and expenses, what you owe other people, and what other people owe you?

____ Have you worked out a way to keep track of your supply inventory so that you will always have enough on hand?

____ Have you figured out how to keep your payroll records and take care of tax reports and payments?

____ Do you know what financial statements you should prepare?

____ Do you know how to use these financial statements?

____ Do you know an accountant who will help you with your records and financial statements?

YOUR BUSINESS AND THE LAW

____ Do you know what licenses and permits you need?

____ Do you know what business laws you have to obey?

____Do you know a lawyer you can go to for advice and for help with legal papers?

PROTECTING YOUR BUSINESS

____Have you made plans for protecting your business against thefts of all kinds--shoplifting, robbery, burglary, employee stealing?

____Have you talked with an insurance agent about what kinds of insurance you need?

BUYING A BUSINESS SOMEONE ELSE HAS STARTED

____ Have you made a list of what you like and do not like about buying a business someone else has started?

____ Are you sure you know the real reason why the owner wants to sell the business?

____ Have you compared the cost of buying the business with the cost of starting a new firm?

____ Are the supplies and inventory in good condition?

____ Is the building in good condition?

____ Will the owner of the building transfer the lease to you?

____ Have you talked with other businesspersons in the area to see what they think of the business?

____ Have you talked with the company's suppliers?

____ Have you talked with a lawyer about it?

CHAPTER XVI
Conclusion

"Never give up on your dream just because it's taking too long for it to become a reality. The time will pass anyway, so you might as well be working on realizing your dream."

M.G.L.J.

MAKING IT GO

ADVERTISING

- ❑ Have you decided how you will advertise? (Newspapers, website, posters, handbills, radio, direct mail, etc.)

- ❑ Do you know where to get help with your ads?

- ❑ Have you watched what other businesses similar to yours do to get people to buy?

THE PRICES YOU CHARGE

- ❑ Do you know how to figure what you should charge for each service you sell?

- ❑ Do you know what other enterprises like yours charge?

BUYING

- ❑ Do you have a plan for finding out what your customers want?

- ❑ Will your plan for keeping track of your inventory tell you when it is time to order more and how much to order?

- ❑ Do you plan to fill most of your needs from a few suppliers rather than a little from many, so that those you buy from will want to help you succeed?

SELLING

- ❑ Do you know how to get customers to buy?

- ❑ Have you thought about why you like to buy from some sales representatives while others turn you off?

YOUR EMPLOYEES

- ❑ If you need to hire someone to help you, do you know where to look?

- ❑ Do you know what kind of person you need?

- Do you know how much to pay?
- Do you have a plan for training your employees?

CREDIT FOR YOUR CUSTOMERS OR CLIENTS

- Have you decided whether to let your customers buy on credit?
- Do you know the advantages and disadvantages of joining a credit card plan?
- Can you tell a deadbeat from a good credit customer?

A FEW EXTRA QUESTIONS

- Have you figured out whether you could make more money working for someone else?
- Does your family support your plan to start a business of your own?
- Do you know where to find out about new ideas and new services?
- Do you have a work plan for yourself and your employees?[19]
- Have you considered business regulations and insurance? Please reflect on the following.

REGULATIONS

Every potential business owner must become familiar with the different business regulations and laws affecting her or his type of business and, specifically, her or his area as they vary from locality to locality. These laws change from time to time so it is necessary to obtain current information for your locality. The licenses and permits required to start a business vary among cities, counties and states. The individual considering entrepreneurship should consult local government agencies or the local Chamber of Commerce for this type of information.

INSURANCE

Many businesses fail each year due to natural disasters, fire, damage suits, burglary, death of a partner, vandalism, employee theft, fraud, etc. Different types of insurance exist which can cover all of these different situations to minimize these risks. It is best to contact a reputable insurance company for your particular needs. Five kinds of insurance are essential: fire insurance, liability insurance, automobile insurance, workers' compensation, and crime insurance. Based on your particular business, you may need many additional types of insurance coverage. A good insurance company will be able to advise you as to appropriate coverage. Also, consult a good attorney for advice on the appropriate insurance coverage for your business.

The operation of the proposed venture must be examined to determine if the sale of the product or service at certain cost levels seems feasible. The following concerns should be considered:

1. What are the major difficulties in the sale of the product or delivery of the service being considered?

2. Why do you think you can sell the venture's product or operate your service at competitive cost level?

3. Discuss the layout of your firm in terms of physical facilities.

4. Thoroughly consider and discuss all major risks and problems and address the minimization of the serious risks.

If you decide that your business is feasible, additional steps need to be taken in order to officially begin operations.

You should.....

- Obtain a business license from the city and/or county clerk.
- Obtain an employee federal identification number from the nearest Internal Revenue Service Office.
- Obtain an application for a sales and use tax certificate of registration.
- Comply with appropriate local, state and federal regulations.

- State laws require employers to cover employees with workers' compensation insurance. Contact the State Department of Labor and obtain the form "First Report of Work Insurance" to determine your state requirements.

- Comply with your State Division of Occupational and Health Association even if you employ only one person.

- Determine if certification by an appropriate board is necessary for your business.

- Contact your State Regulatory Board for more details.

- Check into local permits and ordinances.

- Check with your local or state Small Business Office or local Small Business Development Center to make sure you are in compliance with the regulations for your state and local municipality.

POINTERS FOR BUSINESS SUCCESS

This writer would like to close this publication with a few last pointers for small business success.

1. Develop a "total product" desired by the appropriate target market.

2. Please your customers.

    - Learn their likes and dislikes and make them feel that you are interested.

    - Given an extra bit of service, people will tell others.

    - It is the little things that count and that give your clients or customers that "warm and fuzzy" feeling, and keeps them coming back.

    - Tell the truth about your service even if it means losing a sale. Telling the truth will make that "would be" customer feel that you are an honest businessperson, and they will perhaps patronize you later or tell others.

    - Build an image.

    - Use a steady promotion plan and be consistent in everything you do.

3. Encourage teamwork.

    - Make employees feel that they are important to your business.

    - Praise employees in public; correct them in private.

    - Send your staff to workshops and seminars periodically. The knowledge obtained will allow them to benefit your organization more; and at the same time, it will elevate their feeling of worth to you and your organization.

4. Plan ahead.

5. Keep expenses in line and make a profit. Determine your break-even point.

6. Be involved in civic and community affairs. This is free advertising. Do benevolent

community deeds which will bring a positive valence to your firm.

7. Keep your firm's name in the public's eye.

- Always carry your business cards and brochures.
- Have your business checks imprinted with your logo and a descriptive statement about your business. Checks pass through the hands of many individuals who may be in your target market.

8. Interact and socialize with people who can help you with your business concerns. "It's not what you know; it's who you know." This is an old cliche, but it is quite true in the world of small business. Particularly get to know a banker, lawyer, accountant, marketing/promotion specialist, local politicians, news media representatives, leaders of business, civic, service, political, educational, religious, and professional organizations, and the decision makers of the companies with whom you do business. You may also want to consider joining your local Chamber of Commerce.

9. Establish yourself as an authority in your field or industry. Use your contacts and get on the guest lecture circuit, talk shows and community programs. You may even want to teach a class in your field as a part of the continuing education program of a local college. You may have to offer your teaching free initially, but the benefits derived will be great.

10. Establish credibility for your business.

11. Provide a good service at an acceptable price and back up your product with

12. guarantees and warranties.

13. Live up to the commitments you make.

14. Surround yourself with people who know more than you do. Hire staff personnel whose areas of expertise will enable you to expand your knowledge as well as expand your business.

15. Establish and maintain good credit.

16. Pay your bills on time. If you can't pay on time, call your creditor and see what other arrangements can be made. (These bills will not disappear, so face up to the problem which is quite common for small businesses.)

17. Take advantage of early payment discounts and quantity discounts whenever possible.

18. Always represent your business in a very professional manner.

    - You are your business, and people will evaluate your business based on you. Your personal appearance is very important at all times even on Saturday morning in the grocery store.

    - Always wear clothes that are appropriate for your business field and that make you feel that you look good. You feel and act like you look.

    - When greeting people, always use a firm, confident handshake with direct eye contact and a friendly smile.

19. Keeping cash flow concerns in mind, establish a feasible credit policy for customers and clients.

CHAPTER XVII

Business Glossary

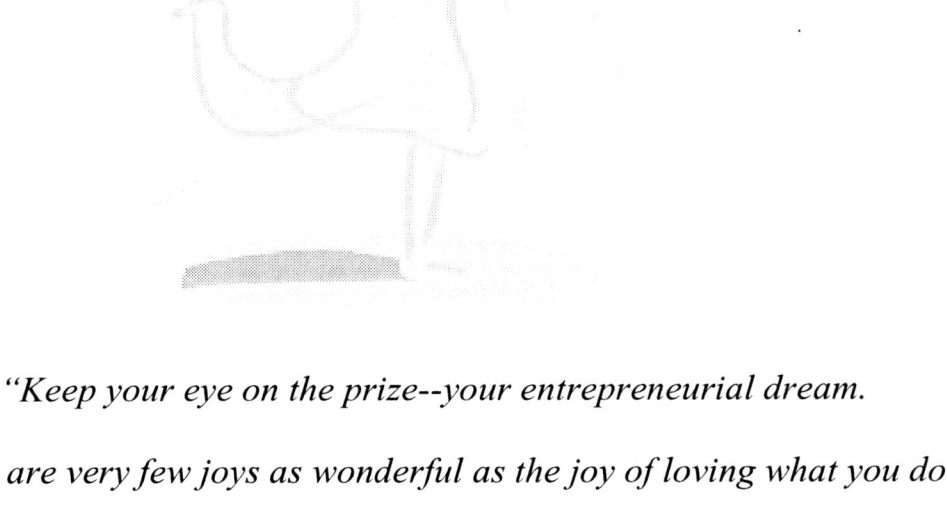

"Keep your eye on the prize--your entrepreneurial dream. There are very few joys as wonderful as the joy of loving what you do every day and getting paid for it."

M.G.L.J.

BUSINESS GLOSSARY

ANGELS	People who may be willing to supply capital to an entrepreneur with no strings attached. These individuals may include relatives, friends or a mentor.
ASSETS	An item of value owned by a business or individual.
BALANCE SHEET	A financial statement which lists the firm's assets and liabilities. It shows what the business is worth.
BALLOON PAYMENT	A final payment generally on an installment loan that is larger than the preceding payment.
BANKRUPT	The state of a person or firm unable to pay creditors and judged legally insolvent.
BOND	A long-term instrument used to finance the capital needs of a business or government unit.
BREAK-EVEN POINT	The volume of sales at which the firm's costs equal its income. Above the break-even point a firm is making money. Below the break-even point a firm is losing money.
BROKER	An agent who negotiates contracts of purchase or sale but does not take control of the goods.
BUDGET	An itemized summary of probable expenditures and income for a given period of time with a plan for meeting expenses.
BUSINESS PLAN	Document prepared by the business owners which details specific information about the firm.
BUYER	The person who makes the purchase decisions for a firm.
COLLATERAL	Property, stocks, bonds, savings accounts, life insurance and current business assets which may be held to insure repayment of a loan.
CAPITAL	Cash or cash equivalents necessary to fund a business entity.

CAPITAL ASSET	An asset with a life of more than one year that is not bought and sold in the ordinary course of business activity.
CAPITAL BUDGETING	The process of planning expenditures on assets whose returns are expected to extend beyond one year.
CAPITAL GAIN (LOSSES)	Profits (or losses) on the sale of capital assets owned for six months or more.
CASH FLOW	A financial projection utilized by business owner(s) to evaluate receipts and disbursements over time. A cash forecast is used to predict high and low points in regard to profitability.
CASH FLOW PROJECTION	Forecast of the cash a business anticipates receiving and distributing during the course of a given span of time.
CASH MANAGEMENT	The practice of using the firm's money to earn money rather than allowing it to remain in accounts which do not pay interest.
COMMERCIAL BANK	An ordinary bank of deposit and discount, with checking accounts, as distinguished from a savings bank.
COMMON STOCK	The ownership element of a corporation represented by shares of stock.
COMPETITIVE EDGE	A particular characteristic (or characteristics) which makes a firm and/or product more attractive to customers than its competitors.
CONSIGNMENT	Goods placed by the supplier in the inventory of the consignee. The consignee pays the supplier only when goods are sold.
CONSUMER GOODS	Goods which are bought by the final user.
CONSUMER PRODUCT SAFETY COMMISSION	A federal commission with responsibility for establishing product safety standards and for taking appropriate steps to reduce unreasonable risks of injury or harm to consumers.
CONTINGENCY FUND	Monies set aside for unexpected expenditures.

CORPORATION	A form of business ownership which is considered a legal entity separate and distinct from the owner.
COST-BENEFIT ANALYSIS	An analytic technique of weighing the costs of a project or investment against the benefits derived therefrom.
COTTAGE INDUSTRY	Another term for the home-based business industry.
CPA	Certified Public Accountant.
CREDIT POLICIES	The firm's customer-payment policies.
DEBT CAPITAL	Monies loaned to the business owner which is used to increase and enhance the value of the firm. The money plus interest must be repaid over time and represents a debt for the firm.
DEBT FINANCING	Funds borrowed for certain business purposes and which must be repaid by the business to the lender.
DECENTRALIZATION	The degree to which decision making has been delegated downward in the organization.
DISPOSABLE INCOME	Personal income remaining after the deduction of taxes on personal income and other compulsory payments.
DROP SHIPMENT	The delivery of goods directly from a producer or wholesaler to the consumer.
DUN & BRADSTREET	A mercantile agency which offers credit ratings, financial analysis, and other financial services, usually on a contractual basis.
EBIT	Earnings before interest and taxes.
EMPLOYEE TURNOVER	The rate at which employees are hired and terminated, or leave the organization.
ENTREPRENEUR	A person who organizes, manages, and initiates a business venture.

EQUITY	The net worth of a business which consists of capital stocks, capital (or paid-in) surplus, earned surplus (or retained earnings) and, sometimes, certain net worth reserves. When capital is provided for business use by an outside person or persons or institutions who become part owners in the firm.
EQUITY CAPITAL	Money obtained by selling a part of the interest in your business
FRANCHISOR	The owner of the product or service in a franchising relationship.
FRANCHISEE	The affiliated dealer through which a franchisor distributes products or services.
FRANCHISING	A form of licensing by which the owner of a product, service or process obtains distribution at the retail level through affiliated dealers.
FIXED ASSETS	Assets of a business which are relatively permanent and are necessary for the functioning of the firm. Fixed assets include buildings, furniture, equipment, etc.
FIXED COSTS	Costs which remain constant regardless of changes in output. Fixed costs include interest on long-term loans, rents, salaries, etc.
FOB (FREE ON BOARD)	The point at which the title of goods transfers (free on board) from the producer to the buyer. FOB origin means that the title is transferred upon leaving the loading dock of the producer and that the shipping costs are paid by the buyer.
GENERAL PARTNERSHIP	A partnership arrangement in which each partner is held liable for the acts of other partners.
GOOD FAITH	A sincere belief that the accomplishment intended is not unlawful or harmful to another.
GOODS-IN-PROCESS	Goods in the midst of production or manufacture such that they are neither in a raw material state nor finished.

GOODWILL	Intangible asset based on the good image of a firm and established by the excess of the price paid for the going concern over its book value.
GROSS INCOME	Amount received by the firm before deducting operating expenses.
HOME BASED BUSINESS	A business primarily operating out of the owner's or owners' home(s).
IMPULSE GOODS	Goods bought by consumers on sight to satisfy a desire that is strongly felt at the moment.
INVENTORY	The total of items of tangible property which a firm uses up or sells during a short time, including goods, material, supplies and tools.
INVESTMENT PROSPECTUS	A document which highlights the major information regarding a business. This document summarizes information so that potential investors can quickly and easily evaluate a business venture.
INVESTMENT TAX CREDIT	A credit from federal income taxes that is computed as a percentage of the initial cost of certain capital assets.
JOBBER	A wholesaler or distributor.
LIABILITY	A debt or obligation of a business.
LIMITED PARTNER	The liability of the limited partner is limited to the amount he or she contributes to the enterprise owned.
LIMITED PARTNERSHIP	A partnership arrangement which is created by compliance with a state's statutory requirements. It is composed of one or more persons.
LINE AND STAFF	A descriptive term which defines the structure of an organization. Line refers to jobs or roles which have direct authority and responsibility for output. Staff personnel contribute indirectly or support line personnel.

LINE OF CREDIT	An arrangement whereby a financial institution commits itself to lend to a firm or individual up to a specified maximum amount of funds during a specified period.
LIQUIDATION	The process of terminating a firm's existence by selling its assets and paying its debts.
LIQUIDITY	A firm's cash position and its ability to meet maturing obligations.
LOSS LEADER	A product priced at a loss or no profit for the purpose of attracting patronage to a store.
MBO (MANAGEMENT BY OBJECTIVES)	A management technique of defining attainable goals for subordinates through an agreement of (MBO) the supervisor and subordinates. It offers continual feedback to subordinates in terms of their contribution to the organization's total performance.
MANUFACTURER'S AGENT	An agent who generally operates on an extended contractual basis, often sells a definite portion of the principal's output within an exclusive territory, handles noncompeting but related lines of goods, and possesses limited authority with regard to prices and terms of sales.
MARKDOWN	A reduction in selling price. (An item priced at $1 would have a 30 percent markdown if it were discounted to a special price of $0.70.)
MARKET SEGMENTATION	A marketing strategy consciously developed to produce a product or service that embodies characteristics preferred by a selected small part of a total market.
MARKET SHARE	The percentage of the total market that the firm can obtain.
MARKETING	Activities concerned with the sale and distribution of a firm's products or services according to needs of customers.
MARKETING CHANNEL	The pipeline through which a product flows on its way to the ultimate consumer.

MARKETING CONCEPT	The way in which a firm chooses to give special consideration to the needs, desires and wishes of prospective and present customers.
MARKETING MIX	A blend in the proper proportions of the basic elements of product, price, promotion and place into an integrated marketing program.
MARKETING PLAN	A plan which details the marketing activity and marketing direction a firm plans to take.
MISSION	The long-term vision of what the firm is trying to become.
NET PROFIT	The amount earned by the firm after paying operating expenses and taxes.
NET WORTH	The difference between assets and liabilities.
OBJECTIVES	Purposes, goals and desired results for the company and its parts.
ODD PRICING	Setting the price of goods to end in an odd number (such as $9.95).
OPERATING EXPENSES	General expenses incurred by the business to generate sales.
OVERHEAD	All the costs of a business other than direct labor and materials.
OWNER'S EQUITY	The amount of cash or other assets the owner has invested in the business.
PARTNERSHIP	The joining of two or more individuals to form an organization.
PAYBACK PERIOD	The length of time required for the net revenues of an investment to equal the cost of the investment.
POLICIES	Overall guides for action and decision making to provide some consistency in company operations.
PREFERRED STOCK	A type of company financing that has characteristics of both bonds and common stock.

PRICE/ EARNINGS RATIO	The ratio of price per share to earnings per share.
PRIVATE BRAND	A brand sponsored by a merchant (e.g. Kroger) or agent as distinguished from brands sponsored by manufacturers or producers.
PRODUCT LINE	A group of products that are closely related because they satisfy a class of needs, are used together, are sold to the same customer groups, are marketed through the same type of outlet or fall within a given price range.
PROFIT-LOSS STATEMENT	Also called the Income Statement, this financial statement lists the total sales, cost of goods sold, expenses, and taxes required in order to obtain a profit (usually for a period of a month).
PROMOTION	A blend of the three following sales activities: (1) mass, impersonal selling efforts (advertising), (2) personal sales, and (3) other activities, such as point-of-purchase displays, shows or exhibits.
PROPRIETORSHIP	An enterprise owned by one individual. The owner and the business are one and the same and cannot be legally distinguished and separated by law.
RETAILER	A merchant or agent whose main business is to buy goods for resale to the ultimate consumer.
SAVINGS AND LOAN BANK	A bank which accepts and pays interest on deposit savings, subject to conditions prescribed by the Federal Home Loan Bank Board.
SBA	Small Business Administration. The SBA is the major governmental agency formulated to assist small businesses.
SBDC	Small Business Development Center. SBDCs are established to provide free management assistance to small business owners.

SERVICE BUSINESS	A firm filling non-product needs of customers. (Examples are banking and repairing firms.)
SILENT PARTNER	An investor who does not have any management responsibilities but provides capital and share liability for any losses experienced by the entity. Also known as a sleeping partner.
SPAN OF CONTROL	The number of subordinates reporting to one supervisor in an organization.
SPECIALTY GOODS	Items which are bought infrequently at particular outlets after a special effort.
STRATEGY	A plan of action to attain specified objectives.
STRATEGIC PLAN	A major, comprehensive, long-term plan providing direction for a firm to accomplish its mission and objectives.
TARGET MARKET	The group of people to whom a firm directs its marketing efforts.
TRADE ASSOCIATION	An organization formed to benefit members of the same trade by informing and supporting its members.
TRADE CREDIT	Interfirm debt arising through credit sales and recorded as an account receivable by the seller and as an account payable by the buyer.
TRADEMARK	A name or logo which is given legal protection because it refers exclusively to a product. It may be used only by the trademark owner.
UNDER-CAPITALIZATION	The lack of funds necessary to optimally start and operate a venture.
UNITY OF COMMAND	The theory that an employee should have only one superior to whom he or she is directly responsible for certain matters.
VENTURE CAPITAL	Cash or cash equivalents supplied by an outside party who specializes in providing working capital for small and/or growing businesses. Venture capitalists require an equity interest in the firm in return for supplying capital assistance.

WHOLESALER	A business unit which buys and resells merchandise to retailers and other merchants and/or to industrial, institutional and commercial users but which does not sell in significant amounts to ultimate consumers.
WORKING CAPITAL	Current assets less current liabilities.

CHAPTER XVIII

Business Resources

"By perseverance, the tortoise won the race."

M.G.L.J.

CHILD CARE RESOURCES

ASSOCIATIONS AND SERVICES

American Associate Degree Early Childhood Educators (ACCESS)
1901 N. Moore Ave.
Moore, OK 737160
http://www.accessece.org
- Publication:
  ACCESS Newsletter (twice a year)

Board on Children, Youth, and Families (BOCYF)
National Research Council/Institute of Medicine
500 5th Avenue NW, 11th Floor
Washington, DC 20001
Phone: 202/334-1935
Fax: 202/334-3829
http://www7.nationalacademies.org/bocyf/index.html
- Publication:
  Children and Families E-News (monthly email)

Center for Early Childhood Leadership (CECL)
National-Louis University
6310 Capitol Dr.
Wheeling, IL 60090-7201
Phone: 800/443-5522 ext. 7703
http://www2.nl.edu/twal/
- Publication:
  Director's Link (quarterly)

Center for Innovations in Special Education (CISE)
University of Missouri-Columbia, Department of Special Education
Ste. 152 Parkade Center, Business Loop 70 W.
Columbia, MO 65211-8020
Phones: 800/976-2473 (MO only), 573/884-7275
TDD: 800/735-2966
http://www.coe.missouri.edu/~mocise/
- Publications:
  The Buzz (quarterly)
  First Steps News
  Innovations
  PARAdise News

Center for the Child Care Work Force
555 New Jersey Avenue, N.W.
Washington, DC 20001
Phone: 202/662-8005
Fax: 202/662-8006
http://www.ccw.org/
- Publications:
  http://www.ccw.org/tpp/index.html

The Child Care Law Center (CCLC)
221 Pine Street, 3rd Floor
San Francisco, CA 94104
Phone: 415/394-7144
Fax: 415/394-7140
http://www.childcarelaw.org
- Publication: *Legal Update* (quarterly)

Child Development Associate National Credentialing Program
1341 Fourth Street, N.W., Suite 802
Washington, D.C. 20005
Phone: (202) 265-9090
- Publication: *Competence* (newsletter)

Child Trends
4301 Connecticut Ave. NW, Ste. 100
Washington, DC 20008
Phone: 202/572-6000
Fax: 202/362-5533
http://www.childtrends.org/
- Publication: *Child Indicator* (3 times a year)

Children's Defense Fund (CDF)
25 E Street NW
Washington, DC 20001
Phone: 202/628-8787
http://www.childrensdefense.org/

The Children's Foundation (CF)
725 15th St. NW, Ste. 505
Washington, DC 20005-2109
Phone: 202/347-3300
Fax: 202/347-3382
http://www.childrensfoundation.net/

Comprehensive Day Care Programs (CDCP)
Spring Garden at 13th St.
Philadelphia, PA 19123
Phone: (215) 351-7200.

Council for Early Childhood Professional Recognition (CECPR)
Washington, DC 20005
Phone: (202)265-9090
Publications: (1) Competence (3/year. Newsletter)
(2) Essentials
(3) Improving Day care Through the Child Development Associate

The Council for Exceptional Children (CEC)
1110 N. Glebe Rd., Ste. 300
Arlington, VA 22201-5704
Phones: 888/232-7733, 703/620-3660
TTY(text only): 866/915-5000
Fax: 703/264-9494
http://www.cec.sped.org/
Publications:
Teaching Exceptional Children (bimonthly)
Exceptional Children (quarterly)

Council on Accreditation for Children and Family Services (COA)
120 Wall St. 11th Fl.
New York, NY 10005
Phone: 212/797-3000 or 800/COA-8088
Fax: 212/797-1428
http://www.coanet.org/

The Division for Early Childhood (DEC)
634 Eddy Avenue
Missoula, MT 59812
Phone: 406/243-5898
Fax: 406/243-4730
Email: dec@selway.umt.edu
http://www.dec-sped.org/
Publications:
Journal of Early Intervention (quarterly)
Young Exceptional Children (quarterly)

ERIC Clearinghouse on Elementary and Early Childhood Education (ERIC/EECE)
University of Illinois, Children's Research Center
51 Gerty Dr.
Champaign, IL 61820-7469
Phone: 800/583-4135
TTY/voice: 217/333-1386
Fax: 217/333-3767
http://ericeece.org/
Publications:
Early Childhood Research & Practice (ECRP)
ERIC/EECE Newsletter (twice a year)

International Association for the Child's Right to Play (IPA)
Box 7701, NCSU
Raleigh, NC 27695-7701
Phone: (919) 737-2204
Publications:
(1) International Play Journal (periodic)
(2) PlayRights (quarterly. Magazine)
(3) also publishes conference proceedings

National Academy of Early Childhood Programs
1509 16th St. NW
Washington, DC 20036-1426
Phone: 202/232-8777, 800/424-2460 ext.11360
Fax: 202/232-1720
http://www.naeyc.org/accreditation/default.asp
Publication: *Accreditation Update*

National Association for Family Day Care
P.O. Box 71268
Murray, VT 84107
Phone: (215) 622-0663
Publications:
(1) National Perspective
(2) What is Family Day Care

National Association for Gifted Children
1707 L St. NW, Ste. 550
Washington, DC 20036
Phone: 202/785-4268
Fax: 202/785-4248
http://www.nagc.org
    Publication: *Gifted Child Quarterly*

National Association for Multicultural Education (NAME)
733 15th St. NW, Ste. 430
Washington, DC 20005
Phone: 202/628-6263
Fax: 202/628-6264
http://www.nameorg.org
    Publications:
    Multicultural Perspectives (quarterly)
    NAME News (quarterly)

National Association for Sick Child Daycare (NASCD)
1716 5th Ave. N.
Birmingham, AL 35203
Phone: 205/324-8447
Fax: 205/324-8050
http://www.nascd.com/
    Publication: *National Association for Sick Child Daycare* (quarterly)

National Association for the Education of Young Children (NAEYC)
1509 16th St. NW
Washington, DC 20036-1426
Phones: 800/424-2460, 202/232-8777
Fax: 202/328-1846
http://www.naeyc.org
    Publications:
    Early Childhood Research Quarterly
    Young Children (bimonthly)

National Association of Child Care Professionals (NACCP)
P.O. Box 90723
Austin, TX 78709-0723
Phone: 512/301-5557
Hotline: 800/537-1118
Fax: 512/301-5080
http://www.naccp.org
    Publications:
    Caring for Your Children© (quarterly)
    Early Childhood News (bimonthly)
    Professional Connections ™
    TeamWork©

National Association of Child Care Resource and Referral Agencies (NACCRRA)
1319 F St. NW, Ste. 500
Washington, DC 20004-1106
Phone: 202/393-5501
Fax: 202/393-1109
http://www.naccrra.net/
    Publication: *The Daily Parent* (quarterly)

National Black Child Development Institute (NBCDI)
1101 15th St. NW, Ste. 900
Washington, DC 20005
Phone: 202/833-2220
Fax: 202/833-8222
http://www.nbcdi.org/
    Publications:
    The Black Child Advocate (2 annually)
    Child Health Talk (2 annually)

National Center for Children in Poverty (NCCP)
215 West 125th Street, 3rd Floor
New York, NY 10027
Phone: 646/284-9600
Fax: 646/284-9623
http://cpmcnet.columbia.edu/dept/nccp/
    Publication: *Child Poverty News & Issues* (3 times a year)

National Center for Early Development & Learning (NCEDL)
UNC-CH CB #8185
Chapel Hill, NC 27599-8185
Phone: 919/966-0867
http://www.fpg.unc.edu/~NCEDL/
   Publication: *NCEDL Newsletter*

National Center for Learning Disabilities (NCLD)
381 Park Ave. S., Ste. 1401
New York, NY 10016
Phones: 888/575-7373, 212/545-7510
Fax: 212/545-9665
http://www.ncld.org/
   Publication: *Our World* (3 times a year)

National Center for Missing and Exploited Children (NCMEC)
Charles B. Wang International Children's Building
699 Prince St.
Alexandria, VA 22314-3175
Hotline: 800/843-5678
Phone: 703/274-3900
Fax: 703/274-2220
http://www.missingkids.org/
   Publication: *The Front Line* (quarterly)

National Child Care Association (NCCA)
1016 Rosser St.
Conyers, GA 30012
Phone: 800/543-7161
http://www.nccanet.org/
   Publication: *The National Focus* (quarterly)

National Child Day Care Association
1501 Benning Road
N.E., Washington, D.C. 20002
Phone: (202) 397-3800

National Coalition for Campus Day Care
c/o UWM Day Care Center
University of Wisconsin-Milwaukee
Milwaukee, WI 53201
Phone: (414)963-5384

National Early Childhood Program Accreditation (NECPA)
126C Suber Road
Columbia, SC 29210
Phone: 800/505-9878
http://www.necpa.net/

National Early Childhood Technical Assistance System (NECTAS)
137 E. Franklin St., Ste. 500
Chapel Hill, NC 27514-3628
Phone: 919/962-2001
TDD: 877/574-3194
Fax: 919/966-7463
http://www.nectas.unc.edu/

National Information Center for Children and Youth with Disabilities (NICHCY)
P.O. Box 1492
Washington, DC 20013
Phone: 800/695-0285
http://www.nichcy.org
   For the various publications see:
   http://www.nichcy.org/pubs1.htm

National Institute for Early Childhood Professional Development (NIECPD)
c/o National Association for the Education of Young Children (NAEYC)
1509 16th St. NW
Washington, DC 20036-1426
Phones: 800/424-2460, 202/232-8777
Fax: 202/328-1846
http://www.naeyc.org/profdev/institute/default.htm

National Latino Children's Institute (NLCI)
1325 North Flores Street, Suite 144
San Antonio, TX 78212
Phone: 210/228-9997
Fax: 210/228-9972
http://www.nlci.org/
   Publication: *EL FUTURO*

National Resource Center for Health and Safety in Child Care (NRCHSCC)
UCHSC at Fitzsimons
Campus Mail Stop F541
P.O. Box 6508
Aurora, CO 80045-0508
Phone: 800/598-5437
Fax: 303/724-0960
http://nrc.uchsc.edu/

Play Schools Association (PSA)
9 E. 38th St., 8th Fl
New York, NY 10016
Phone: (212) 725-6540
    Publications:
    (1) Booklets
    (2) Produces training films

Society for Research in Child Development (SRCD)
University of Chicago Press
5720 Woodlawn Ave.
Chicago, IL 60637
Phone: (312) 702-7470
    Publications:
(1) Child Development Research and Social Policy
(2) Child Development (bimonthly, Journal)
(3) Child Development Abstracts and Bibliography
(3/year. Journal)
(4) Monographs of the Society for Research in Child Development (3-4/year)
(5) Review of Child Development Research
(6) Society for Research in Child Development
(Newsletter, periodic)

The Southern Early Childhood Association (SECA)
P.O. Box 55930
Little Rock, AR 72215-5930
Phone: 800/305-7322
Fax: 501/227-5297
http://southernearlychildhood.org
    Publication: *Dimensions of Early Childhood*

U.S. National Committee of the World Organization for Early Childhood Education (OMEP-USNC)
c/o OMEP-USNC Treasurer
Dept. of Curriculum & Instruction MC 4610
Southern Illinois University
Carbondale, IL 62901-4610
http://omep-usnc.org/
    Publications:
    International Journal of Early Childhood
    OMEP-USNC Newsletter

U.S.A. Toy Library Associate (USA-TLA)
2530 Crawford Ave., Ste. 111
Evanston, IL 60201-4954
Phone (708) 864-3330
    Publications:
    (1)Child's Play (quarterly, newsletter)
    (2) Directory of Toy Libraries in the U.S.
    (3) Play is a Child's Work. (video)
    (4) Toy Library Operators Manual(periodic)

Wheelock College Institute for Leadership and Career Initiatives
(formerly Center for Career Development in Early Care and Education)
Wheelock College
200 The Riverway
Boston, MA 02215
Phone: 617/734-5200, ext. 211
Fax: 617/738-0643
http://institute.wheelock.edu/

World Organization for Human Potential (WOHP)
8801 Stenton Ave.
Philadelphia, PA 19118
Phone: (215) 233-2050

Zero to Three: National Center for Infants, Toddlers, and Families
2000 M St. N.W., Ste. 200
Washington, DC 20036
Phone: 202/638-1144
http://www.zerotothree.org/
    Publication: *Zero to Three* (bimonthly)

GOVERNMENT AGENCIES

Administration for Children, Youth, and Families (ACYF)
http://www.acf.dhhs.gov/programs/acyf/acyf.htm

Child Care Bureau
U.S. Department of Health and Human Services
Administration for Children, Youth, and Families
Switzer Bldg., Rm. 2046
330 C St., SW
Washington, DC 20447
    Phone: 202/690-6782
    Fax: 202/690-5600
    http://www.acf.dhhs.gov/programs/ccb/

National Child Care Information Center (NCCIC)
243 Church St., NW, 2nd Fl.
Vienna, VA 22180
Phone: 800/616-2242
Fax: 800/716-2242
TTY: 800/516-2242
http://nccic.org/
    Publication: *Child Care Bulletin* (yearly)

National Institute on Early Childhood Development and Education (ECI)
Office of Educational Research and Improvement
U.S. Department of Education
555 New Jersey Ave. NW
Washington, DC 20208
Phone: 202/219-1935
Fax: 202/273-4768
http://www.ed.gov/offices/OERI/ECI/
    Publications:
    Early Childhood Digest (quarterly)
    Early Childhood Update

U.S. Department of Education (ED)
400 Maryland Ave. SW
Washington, DC 20202-0498
Phone: 800/872-5327
http://www.ed.gov/

U.S. Department of Health and Human Services (HHS)
200 Independence Ave. SW
Washington, DC 20201
Phones: 877/696-6775, 202/619-0257
http://www.dhhs.gov/

PUBLICATIONS

Child Care Information Exchange
P.O. Box 3249
Redmond, WA 98073-3249
Phone: 800/221-2864
http://www.ccie.com/

Child Care Provider
12435 Kemmerton Ln.
Bowie, MD 20715
Phone: 301/262-0274

Healthy Child Care
Healthy Child Publications
P.O. Box 624
Harbor Springs, MI 49740
Phone: 616/526-6342
Fax: 616/526-0428
http://www.healthychild.net/index.html

Healthy Child Care America
American Academy of Pediatrics
P.O. Box 927
Elk Grove Village, IL 60009-0928
Phone: 800/433-9016, ext. 7132

WEB SITES

The ABC's of Safe and Healthy Child Care
http://www.cdc.gov/ncidod/hip/ABC/abc.htm

Early Learning Information Online Together (ELIOT)
http://www.eliot.org/

National Child Care Information Center's List of Child Care Resources on the World Wide Web
http://nccic.org/pubs.html

National Network for Child Care (NNCC)
http://www.nncc.org/

NATIONAL BUSINESS ASSOCIATIONS

AMERICAN ASSOCIATION OF BLACK WOMEN ENTREPRENEURS, INC.
P. O. BOX 7460
SILVER SPRING, MD 20907

AMERICAN BUSINESS WOMEN'S ASSOCIATION
P. O. BOX 8728
9100 WARD PARKWAY
KANSAS CITY, MO 64114   (816) 361-6621

AMERICAN ENTREPRENEURS ASSOCIATION
2311 PONTIUS AVENUE
LOS ANGELES, CA 90064   (213) 478-0437

INTERNATIONAL ASSOCIATION FOR HOME BUSINESSES
P. O. BOX 14460
CHICAGO, IL 60614

NATIONAL ALLIANCE OF HOME-BASED BUSINESS WOMEN
P. O. BOX 306
MIDLAND PARK, NJ 07432

NATIONAL ASSOCIATION OF WOMEN BUSINESS OWNERS
645 N. MICHIGAN
CHICAGO, IL 60611

BOOKS

Adams, Rob (2002). A Good Kick in the Ass. New York: Crown Business.

Alarid, William, Berle, Gustav (1997). Free Help From Uncle Sam to Start Your Own Business (Or Expand the One You Have), 4th ed. Santa Maria, CA: Puma Pub. Company.

Applegate, Jane (1998). 201 Great Ideas For Your Small Business. New York: Bloomberg Press.

Bean, Roger, Radford, Russell (2000). Powerful Products: Strategic Management of Successful New Product Development. New York: AMACOM

Berry, Tim (1998). Hurdle: The Book on Business. Eugene, Oregon: Palo Alto Software, Inc.

Birkeland, Peter M (2002). Franchising Dreams: the Lure of Entrepreneurship in America. Chicago: University of Chicago Press.

Birkinshaw, Julian (2000). Entrepreneurship in the Global Firm. Thousand Oaks, CA: SAGE Publication.

Birley, Sue (1998). Entrepreneurship. Brookfield, VT: Ashgate.

Boston, Thomas D. and Century Foundation (1999). Affirmative Action and Black Entrepreneurship. London, New York: Routledge.

Butler, John (2001). E-Commerce and Entrepreneurship. Greenwich, Conn: Information Age Publishers.

Burgess, Stephen (2002). Managing Information Technology in Small Business: Challenges and Solutions. Hershey, PA: Idea Group Publication.

Canefield, Jack, and Hansen, Mark Victor, and Hewitt Les (2000). The Power of Focus: How to Hit Your Business, Personal and Financial Targets with Absolute Certainty. Deerfield Beach, FL: Health Communications, Inc.

Carey, Charles W. (2002). American Inventors, Entrepreneurs, and Business Visionaries. New York: Facts on File.

Cartwright, Roger and NetLibrary, Inc. (2002). The Entrepreneurial Individual. Oxford, UK: Capstone Pub.

Cheney, Karen and Alderman, Lesley (1997). How to Start a Successful Home Business. New York: Warner Books.

Cleaver, Joanne Y. (1999). Find & Keep Customers for Your Small Business. Chicago, IL: CCH Incorp.

Coulter, Mary (2001). Entrepreneurship in Action. New Jersey: Prentice Hall.

Crainer, Stuart (2000). Generation Entrepreneur: Shape Today's Business Reality, Create Tomorrow's Wealth, Do Your Own Thing. London: Financial Times Prentice Hall.

Da Costa, Eduardo (2001). Global E-Commerce Strategies for Small Business. Cambridge, Mass: MIT Press.

Debelak, Don (2001). Think Big: Nine Ways to Make Millions from Your Ideas. Irvine, CA: Entrepreneur Press.

Dees, J. Gregory, Emerson, Jed, and Economy, Peter (2002). Strategic Tools for Social Entrepreneurs: Enhancing the Performance of Your Enterprising Nonprofit. Somerset, NJ: John Wiley and Sons, Inc.

DeLuca, Fred and Hayes, John Phillip (2000). Start Small, Finish Big: Fifteen Key Lessons To Start –and Run—Your Own Successful Business. New York: Warner Books.

Fick, David S. (2002). Entrepreneurship in Africa, A Study of Success. Westport, Connecticut: Quorum Books.

Foley, James F (1999). The Global Entrepreneur: Taking Your Business International. Chicago: Dearborn.

Galambos, Louis and Abrahamson, Eric John (2002). Anytime, Anywhere: Entrepreneurship and the Creation of a Wireless World. Cambridge, New York: Cambridge University Press.

Gerber, Michael E. (1995). The E-Myth Revisited: Why Most Small Business Don't Work and What to Do About It. New York: Harper Collins Publishers.

Goltz, Jay with Oesterricher, Judy (1998). The Street-Smart Entrepreneur: 133 Tough Lessons I Learned the Hard Way. Omaha, NB: Addicus Books.

Gravely, Melvin J (1995). The Black Entrepreneur's Guide to Success. Edgewood, MD: Duncan & Duncan.

Gravely II, Melvin J. (1997). Making It Your Business: The Personal Transition from Employee to Entrepreneur. Cincinnati, OH: Impact Group Consultants.

Hall, Doug (2001). Jump Start Your Business Brain. Cincinnati, OH: Brain Brew Books.

Hayes, Cassandra (2002). Black Enterprise Guide to Building Your Career. New York: John Wiley.

Hisrich, Robert D and Peters, Michael P. (1995). Entrepreneurship: Starting, Developing, and Managing A New Enterprise 3rd ed. Chicago: Irwin.

Hitt, Michael A. (2002). Strategic Entrepreneurship: Creating A New Integrated Mindset. Malden, MA: Blackwell.

Inman, Katherine (2000). Women's Resources in Business Start-up: A Study of Black and White Women Entrepreneurs. New York: Garland Publisher.

Janal, Daniel S. (1997). 101 Successful Businesses You Can Start on the Internet. New York: Van Nostrand Reinhold.

Johnson, Van R. (2000). Entrepreneurial Management and Public Policy. Huntington, NY: Nova Science Publishers.

Kijakazi, Kilolo (1997). African-American Economic Development and Small Business Ownership. New York: Garland Pub.

Kotter, John P., Cohen, Dan S. (2002). The Heart of Change: Real-Life Stories of How People Change Their Organizations. Watertown, MA: Harvard Business School Press.

Krass, Peter (1999). The Book of Entrepreneur's Wisdom, Classic Writings by Legendary Entrepreneurs. Somerset, NJ: John Wiley & Sons.

Kuratko, Donald F., Hodgetts, Richard M. (2000). Entrepreneurship: A Contemporary Approach. Fort Worth, TX: Dryden Press.

Lacy, Harold R. (1998). Financing your Business Dreams with Other People's Money: How and Where to Find Money for Start-up and Growing Businesses. Traverse City, MI: Sage Creek Press.

Lane, Marc J. (2001). Advising Entrepreneurs: Dynamic Strategies For Financial Growth. New York: Wiley.

Lipman, Frederick D. (1998). Financing Your Business with Venture Capital: Strategies to Grow Your Enterprise with Outside Investors. Rocklin, CA: Prima.

Lodish, Leonard, Morgan, Howard Lee, and Kallianpur, Amy (2001). Entrepreneurial Marketing: Lessons from Wharton's Pioneering MBA Course. New York: Wiley.

McDaniel, Bruce (2002). Entrepreneurship and Innovation: An Economic Approach. Armonk, NY: M.E. Sharpe.

Meyers, G. Dale, Heppard, Kurt A. (2000). Entrepreneurship As Strategy: Competing on the Entrepreneurial Edge. Thousand Oaks, CA: SAGE Publications, Inc.

Moore, Dorothy P and Buttner, E. Holly (1997). Women Entrepreneurs: Moving Beyond The Glass Ceiling. Thousand Oaks, CA: SAGE Publications.

Murtha, Thomas P., Lenway, Stephanie Ann, and Hart, Jeffrey A. (2003). Managing New Industry Creation: Global Knowledge Formation and Entrepreneurship in High Technology. Palo Alto, CA: Stanford University Press.

Oden, Howard W. (1997). Managing Corporate Culture, Innovation, and Entrepreneurship. Westport, Conn.: Quorum Books.

Ryan, Rob (2001). Smartups. New York: Cornell University Press.

Sexton, Donald L (1999). The Blackwell Handbook of Entrepreneurship. Malden, MA: Blackwell Business.

Sharma, Poonam (1999). The Harvard Entrepreneur's Club Guide to Starting Your Own Business. New York: John Wiley.

Stephenson, James (2001). Entrepreneur's Ultimate Start-up Directory. Irvine, CA: Entrepreneur Press.

Stolze, William (1996). Start Up: An Entrepreneur's Guide to Launching and Managing a New Business. Hawthorne, NJ: Career Press.

Sullivan, Robert (1998). The Small Business Start-Up Guide. Great Falls, VA: Information International.

Sullivan, William R. (1997). Entrepreneur Magazine: Human Resources for Small Business. New York: John Wiley.

Sutton, Garrett et al (2001). Own Your Own Corporation: Why the Rich Own Their Own Companies and Everyone Else Works For Them. New York: Warner Books.

Tabrrok, Alexander (2002). Entrepreneurial Economics: Bright Ideas from the Dismal Science. New York: Oxford University Press.

Turner, Colin (2002). Lead to Succeed: Creating Entrepreneurial Organizations. New York, London: Texere.

Wallace, Robert L (2000). Soul Food: 52 principles of Black Entrepreneurial Success. Cambridge, Mass: Perseus Pub.

Williams, Bernadette (2002). Black Enterprise Guide to Technology for Entrepreneurs. New York: Wiley.

Williams, Edward E and Thompson, James R. (1998). Entrepreneurship and Productivity. Lanham, MD: University Press of America.

Woodard, Michael D (1997). Black Entrepreneurs in America: Stories of Struggle and Success. New Brunswick, NJ: Rutgers University Press.

Young, Ruth C, Francis, Joe D, and Young, Christopher H. (1999). Entrepreneurship, Private and Public. Lanham, MD: University Press of America.

INDEXES

Business Periodicals Index. New York: Wilson.
Subject index to articles in the fields of accounting, advertising, public relations, banking, economics, finance and investments, insurance, labor, management, marketing and taxation. Also includes information on specific businesses, industries and trades.

Readers' Guide to Periodical Literature. New York: Wilson.
Author and subject index to the contents of over 150 general and nontechnical magazines. A good starting point for finding information on a wide variety of topics.
.
Social Sciences and Humanities Index. Vols. 1-27, 1916-1974, formerly called; International Index. Author and subject index to periodicals in the fields of anthropology, economics, environmental science, geography, law and criminology, political science, psychology public administration and sociology.

DICTIONARIES AND ENCYCLOPEDIAS

Middle Market Dictionary. New York: Dun and Bradstreet. Annual. This directory provides information about companies whose net worth ranges from $500,000 to $900,000 including utilities, transportation companies, banks and trust companies, stockbrokers, mutual and stock insurance companies, wholesalers and retailers. The companies are listed alphabetically, geographically and by product classification (S.I.C., Standard Industrial Classification).

Million Dollar Directory. New York: Dun and Bradstreet. Annual. Arranged as is Middle Market Directory. This compilation provides information about companies with a net worth of $1 million or more. It also contains a management directory that lists officers and directors and their affiliations.

Poor's Register of Corporations, Directors and Executives, United States and Canada.
New York: Standard and Poor's Corporation. Annual. Volume I contains alphabetical listing of corporations with directors and executives. Volume 2 is a register of directors and executives of the companies listed in Volume 1. Volume 3 contains Standard Industrial Classification and geographical indexes. Supplements are issued in April, July and October.

List of Small Business Investment Companies. Washington: U.S. Government Printing Office. Irregular.

National Minority Business Directory. Minneapolis: National Minority Business Directories. Annual. This specialized directory lists over 7,000 minority firms (50 percent or more owned by minority group members, classified by product. A cross-reference index aids in finding the appropriate classification. Computer disks are also available. Published by TRY US Resources, Inc. (612) 781-6819.

Thomas Register of American Manufacturers. New York: Thomas Publishing Company. Annual. Manufacturers are arranged according to product, and the manufacturers of each product are listed geographically. Alphabetical indexes to manufacturers, trade names and specific products facilitate its use.

SPECIAL LISTS

Black Enterprise. New York, Monthly. The "top-100". black-owned or managed businesses that gross more than $1 million annually are listed in the June issue each year.

Forbes. New York. Semimonthly. The "Annual Report on American Industry" is in the first issue each year. It lists companies according to profitability, growth and pure stock gain over a five-year period. The "Annual Directory Issue" (May 15) ranks the top 500 corporations in sales, stock market value, assets and profits.

Fortune. New York. Monthly. "The Directory of Largest Corporations" is an annual feature in several parts. The May issue lists the 500 largest U.S. industrial companies by sales. The June issue lists the second-largest 500 U.S. industrial companies. The July issue lists the largest nonindustrial corporations and the fifty largest companies in banking, life insurance, diversified financial services, retailing, transportation and utilities. The August issue lists the largest corporations outside the United States and the September issue lists the 300 largest corporations outside the United States, and the September issue lists the 300 largest banks outside the country.

Encyclopedia of Associations. Detroit: Gale Research. Revised approximately every two years. This classified directory lists over 12,000 organized groups. It lists for each, the address, phone number, chief official, a description, publications and other pertinent information. The alphabetical and key-word index is helpful in locating an association if one does not know its exact name. Supplementary lists of new associations are issued quarterly.

The Foundation Directory. New York: Compiled by the Foundation Center and distributed by Columbia University Press, This directory lists foundations by state. Each entry includes the corporate names, address, purpose, activities and pertinent financial data.

ATLASES AND MAPS

Ginsburg, Norton. Atlas of Economic Development. Chicago: University of Chicago Press. This atlas offers graphic representations of data on population, land resources, transportation, energy generation and consumption. Each map is accompanied by textual material explaining and summarizing the analyzed data.

Rand McNally Commercial Atlas and Marketing Guide. New York: Rand McNally, Annual. Limited to U.S. marketing data, this atlas provides summaries and analyses of statistics by state in the areas of agriculture, manufacturing, population, retail trade and transportation.

BIBLIOGRAPHIES AND GUIDES

Coman, Edwin T. Sources of Business Information. rev. ed. Berkeley and Los Angeles: University of California Press. . The first four chapters of this guide deal with methodology and the range of business sources. The remaining chapters treat such specific fields as accounting, real estate and insurance, and management. Limited to American and Canadian sources, and a few from England.

Encyclopedia of Business Information Sources. 2 vols. Detroit: Gale. Volume I is organized alphabetically by topic, with sub-headings by type of source. Lists primary and secondary sources of information.

PERIODICALS

Academy of Management Journal. Tampa, Fl. Quarterly.

Accounting Review. Sarasota, Fl.: American Accounting Association. Quarterly.

Administrative Science Quarterly. Ithaca, NY.: Cornell University Graduate School of Business and Public Administration. Quarterly.

Black Enterprise. New York. Monthly.

Business Week. New York: McGraw-Hill. Weekly.

Commerce America. Washington: U.S. Department of Commerce. Bi-weekly. Order from U.S. Government Printing Office.

Dun's Review. New York: Dun & Bradstreet. Monthly.

Federal Reserve Bulletin. Washington: U.S. Board of Governors of the Federal Reserve System. Monthly.

Forbes. New York. Semimonthly.

Fortune. New York, Semimonthly.

Harvard Business Review. Boston: Harvard University Graduate School of Business Administration. Monthly.

Industry Week. Cleveland, Ohio: Penton Publishing Company. Weekly.

Money. Chicago. Monthly.

Monthly Labor Review. Washington: U.S. Government Printing Office. Monthly

Nation's Business. Washington: Chamber of Commerce of the United States. Monthly.

Survey of Current Business. Washington: U.S. Department of Commerce. Order from U.S. Government Printing Office. Monthly. Supplemented weekly by Business Statistics.

Wall Street Journal. New York: Dow Jones. 5 issues per week.

CHILD CARE REFERENCES

[1] http://www.womensbusinessresearch.org/Research/5-6-2003/5-6-2003.htm

[2] Population Estimates Program, Population Division, U.S. Census Bureau, Washington, D.C. 20233, Internet Release Date: December 20, 2000.

[3] 2003 **Child Care Center Licensing Study**, The Children's Foundation, Washington, DC

[4] Kenneth Lawyer and Clifford Baumback, How to Organize and Operate a Small Business, 6th Edition (Englewood Cliffs, New Jersey: Prentiuce Hall, 1979, p.56.

[5] Hal B. Pickel, "Personality and Success: An evaluation of Personal Characteristics of Successful Small Business Managers," Small Business Research Series No. 4. Small Business Administration (Washington, DC: G.P.O.), 1964.

[6] Small Business Administration, "Keys to Business Success," Office of Management Assistance (1973), p. 37.

[7] James F. DeCarlo and Paul Lyons, " A Comparison of Selected Personal Characteristics of Minority and Non-Minority Female Entrepreneurs," Journal of Small Business Management, 17 October 1979, pp.25-26.

[8] Ibid, p. 25

[9] Ibid

[10] William Glueck, "Entrepreneurial and Family Firms," Management (Hinsdale, Illinois: Dryden Press, 1977), p. 57.

[11] Ibid, p. 50

[12] Ralph Stogdill, Handbook of Leadership (New York: The Free Press, 1974), pp. 76-82.

[13] Ibid, p. 167

[14] Charles B. Swayne and William R. Tucker, The Effective Entrepreneur (Morristown, NJ: General Learning Press, 1973), p. 35.

[15] *Ibid., p. 35*

[16] Keith Davis, Human Behavior at Work (New York: McGraw Hill, Inc., 1977) p. 26.

[17] Kenneth R. Van Voorhis, Entrepreneurship and Small Business Management (Boston: Allyn & Bacon, 1980), p. 29.

ADDITIONAL GENERAL REFERENCES

http://www.census.gov/epcd/mwb97/us/us.html#Black - Census Bureau info for minority and women owned businesses

http://www.census.gov/prod/ec97/e97cs-2.pdf - consensus info

http://www.census.gov/Press-Release/www/2001/cb01-61.html - women owned businesses numbers from 1997

http://www.nfwbo.org/minority/AllMinority.pdf - Minority women business owners data

Appendix

SAMPLE BUSINESS FORMS

"For all the trials and tears of time, for every hill I have to climb, my heart sings but a grateful song-- these are the things that make me strong."

Anonymous

EXHIBIT A

CHILD'S APPLICATION

_____
Child Care Center, Family Day Care Home, or Group Day Care Home Name

_____
(Address)   (City)   (State)   (Zip)

Date of admission_____ Full name of child_____

Child's birth date_____ Name child likes to be called _____

Parents:

Name of Mother:_____
                     (Last)   (First)

Address:_____ Home Phone:_____

Employer:_____

Work Phone:_____ Work hours:_____

Name of Father:_____
                 (Last)   (First)

Address:_____ Home Phone: _____

Employer:_____

Work Phone:_____ Work hours_____

If parents are divorced, which parent has custody?_____

(For the child's safety, list other persons to whom child may be released.)

_____

_____

Emergency Information:

Name of person, other than operator, authorized to act for parent in an emergency:

_____

Address:_____ Home Phone: _____

Work Phone:_____ Work hours_____

Name of physican::_____

Address:_____ Phone: _____

Background Information:

Other children & adults in the home	Age	School Children Attend
_____	___	_____
_____	___	_____
_____	___	_____

Experiences at School:

What school does child attend?_____

Grade in school_____ Teacher's Name_____

Describe child's adjustment to school:_____

What grades does child make?   Good____   Average____   Poor____

Hobbies:

List child's hobbies and other interests:_____

Experiences with Others:

What are some ways in which the child plays at home?
Does the child play with neighborhood children?_____ If so, how?_____

Does the child usually get own way with other children? _____   If not, how does the child react?_____

Is the entire family together for any time during the day?_____

Has your child had any of the following experiences during the past year?_____

Birth of another child in the family _____
Moving ___
Changing schools ____
Serious illness of child or family member ____
Death in family ____

Separation or divorce of parents ___
Other_____

Would you describe your child as: Active?____ Quiet?____ Friendly?____ Shy?____

What do you like best about your child?_____

Special Permissions:

My child has my permission to go on all field trips arranged by the center. Yes_____ No_____

My child has my permission to leave the center after prior transportation plans are approved for the following purposes: _____

Eating Habits:

At what time does the child eat breakfast?_____ Lunch? ____ Dinner?_____ Between-meal snacks?_____

Does he/she feed himself or herself?_____

What is his/her general attitude toward eating?_____

If he/she refuses to eat, how is this handled and by whom? _____

_____

Favorite foods_____

Disliked foods _____

Foods he/she is allergic to_____

If the child is an infant, use a separate sheet for information about the formula, bottle schedule, etc.

Sleep Habits:

Has own room _____   Shares room with other children____   Rooms with parents_____

At night, sleeps from ____ to ____   Average hours_____

Naps from ____ to ____   Average hours_____

Attitude toward going to bed_____

If there is difficulty, how is this handled?_____

Habits associated with going to bed_____

Does he or she wet the bed?_____ At nap time?_____ At night?____

If so, how is this handled?_____

Toilet Habits:

Time at which child is taken to the bathroom_____

Does the child go by herself or himself?_____   Time of bowel movement?_____ Regular?____

Constipated?_____ Does he/she tell you when they need to go to the toilet and go willingly?_____

Can he or she manage clothes without help at the toilet?____

What word does he or she use for urinating?_____ BM?_____

Speech and Physical Growth:

Does he or she talk well?_____ Fairly well?_____ Indistinctly?_____ Not at all?_____

Does anyone read to him or her?_____   How regularly?_____

At what age did he or she creep?_____   Crawl?_____   Walk?_____

Would you describe your child as active or quiet; thin, average weight, or heavy; tall, average height, or short; friendly or unfriendly?_____

Give below any other information you think we should have about your child:

I do hereby authorize emergency medical care: _____

Signature of Parent(s)

For Internal Use Only

Weekly fee $_____   Monthly fee $_____

Enrolled on_____ Withdrawn on_____ Reason for withdrawal_____

EXHIBIT B

SAMPLE POLICY STATEMENT

_____ CHILD CARE CENTER POLICIES
       Your firm's name

1. The center will be open from _____ a.m. to _____ p.m., Monday through Friday. Children cannot be accepted earlier or kept later. In case of <u>extreme</u> emergency, parent must call the center for child to remain past closing time. A late fee of $_____ will be charged for each _____ minutes you are late.

2. Parents are expected to bring their child into the center and remain within until a brief health check is completed. A child may not remain at the center if he or she is thought to be ill.

3. All enrollment forms for the child must be completed by the parent, and a current immunization record, signed by a health care provider, must accompany the child on admission. Each child must receive all immunizations at entry unless there is a medical reason certified by a health care provider why these immunizations should not be made.

4. Annual health examinations are required and are the responsibility of the parent.

5. If a child becomes ill during the day, his or her parent will be called to come and take him or her home. Sick children cannot be cared for at the center.

6. If a child must be given medication by the center staff, the director must be informed. Each bottle must be clearly labeled with the child's name. A note must be attached with clear instructions for giving the medication.

7. Parents will be promptly notified of the occurrence of a communicable disease among the center's children.

8. Parents are asked to see that children do not bring food, money or toys to the center. Children needing special diets, formula or baby food will be required to provide the necessary items. Unopened jars of baby food are required.

9. Each child must have a change of clothing, clearly marked with his/her name to be left at the center for emergencies. Parents of children requiring diapers must furnish them.

10. Outdoor play is an important part of our program. Please see that your child is suitably dressed to play outside except on extremely bad days.

11. In addition to planned learning and play activities, the following services will be provided by the center:

➢ A hot lunch.
➢ Breakfast.
➢ Morning and afternoon snacks.
➢ Field trips.
➢ Transportation.
➢ Birthday parties.
➢ After-hours care.
➢ Cribs, cots, pads and covers for napping.
➢ Planned parent-teacher conferences.
➢ Planned parent-child activities.

12. Our child care fee is $_____ per week and must be paid in advance each Friday for the following week. Monthly arrangements may also be made for your convenience.

13. The center will be closed on these holidays:
_____
_____
_____
_____
_____
_____

14. Snow Policy.....When the public schools are closed the center will also be closed.

_____   _____
Signature of Center Director   Signature of Parent

Date:_____   Date:_____

Two copies of this statement have been provided for your convenience. Please sign both copies and return one to the center. The other should be kept for your files.

EXHIBIT C

CHILD HEALTH RECORD

Personal Information:

Child's Name_____ Age_____ Sex_____
Birth date_____

Parent's/Guardian's Name_____
Phone No._____ Address_____
City/State/Zip_____

Vaccinations: REQUIRED BEFORE A CHILD IS ACCEPTED FOR CARE.

Please record the number and date of the last dose received.
D.P.T. (Diphtheria-Whooping-Cough-Tetanus)_____

T D (Tetanus-Diphtheria)_____

Rubeola (Measles)_____

Polio_____

Mumps_____

The above information reflects the immunization status according to the best available information of the above named child as of the date of the provider's signature.

Health Provider's Signature or Stamp_____
Date Signed_____

Health Examination: Required only for children under 3 years of age if enrolled in a group infant care center.

This child has been examined. The health history has been reviewed. There are no apparent contraindications to participation in routine group care activities except as stated below.

Comments: (special problems, allergies, etc.)

Examiner's Signature_____ **Date Signed**_____

Examiner's Address _____

Child Health Record:

Optional Services:

TB Skin Test

_____
(Results)   (Date)   (Health Provider's Signature)

Hgb./Hct.

_____
(Results)   (Date)   (Health Provider's Signature)

EXHIBIT D

SAMPLE PURCHASE ORDER FORM

PURCHASE ORDER

Date:_____   P.O. # _____
                                                      (assign in sequence)

TO: (NAME OF SUPPLIER)

How to Ship: (UPS or other)
Terms: (will pay when billed, etc.)

Deliver By: (date needed)

BILL TO: (NAME AND ADDRESS OF FIRM TO RECEIVE BILL)

Shipping & Packing Instructions:

SHIP TO: (NAME AND ADDRESS OF WHERE GOODS SHOULD BE SENT)

Quantity	Item #	Description	Unit Cost	Discount	Total

                    _____
                      GRAND TOTAL

Ordered by:_____

NOTE Please show our order # on all shipments or correspondence, and advise if unable to meet required delivery date.

ANY CHANGES IN THIS PURCHASE ORDER MUST BE IN WRITING

Any such failure that results in documentable third party costs will be deducted from the vendor's invoice. Failure on the part of vendor to meet terms and delivery dates will void this Purchase Order unless such charges are authorized in revised Purchase Order.

EXHIBIT E

BILLING STATEMENT

FIRM NAME, ADDRESS AND CONTACT NUMBERS

Statement Date:_____ **Acct. No.:**_____
(Please refer to this number in all your correspondence)

TO: CUSTOMER NAME

Date	Terms	Items or Services Purchased	Amount	Remarks

Please Pay This Amount: _____

Current	30 days	60 days	90 days and over

*Note: Terms Net _____ Days

EXHIBIT F

PETTY CASH RECORD

DATE	PAID TO	FOR	APPROVED BY	BALANCE ON HAND

EXHIBIT G

BALANCE SHEET

ASSETS

	Present Year	**Prior Year**

Current Assets
   Cash (in hand, in banks)
   Marketable securities
   Accounts receivable (subtract
    allowance for bad debts)
   Inventories
   Prepayments
   Investments (at cost)
   Other _____

Total current assets:

Fixed Assets
   Land
   Buildings
   Machinery
   Office Equipment
   Other _____
    Subtotal
    Less accumulated depreciation
Net fixed assets:
Other assets and deferred charges
Intangibles (goodwill, patents, trademarks)

Total assets

LIABILITIES

Current Liabilities:
   Accounts payable
   Notes payable
   Accrued expenses payable
   Federal and state income taxes payable
   Other _____
Total current liabilities

Long Term Liabilities
   Interest (notes payable after one year)
   Other _____
Total liabilities:

Stockholders' Equity
   Preferred stock
   Common stock
   Accumulated retained earnings
Total stockholders' equity:

Total liabilities and stockholders' equity:

EXHIBIT H

INCOME STATEMENT

	Present Year	Prior Year
Revenues:		
Net sales (operating revenues, less discounts)	_____	_____
Other income:	_____	_____
Total revenue:	_____	_____
Cost of Sales:		
Inventory	_____	_____
Royalties	_____	_____
Other _____	_____	_____
Total cost of sales:	_____	_____
Gross profit or loss:	_____	_____
Operating Expenses		
Selling expense (Adv., payroll, travel, entertainment, etc.)	_____	_____
General administration (Heat, light, rent, etc.)	_____	_____
Other _____	_____	_____
Net income before taxes:	_____	_____
Income taxes:	_____	_____
Net Profit:	_____	_____

A BUSINESS OF YOUR OWN
Business Publications and Services for the Entrepreneurial Woman

"Our purpose is to assist the entrepreneurial woman in pulling together the intricate components necessary to make a small business a success!!!"

FACT SHEET

A BUSINESS OF YOUR OWN is a multifaceted service firm that specializes in business publications and services designed to assist women in starting and managing small businesses.

A BUSINESS OF YOUR OWN publishes information that inspire, motivate, educate and help the female entrepreneur grow and develop skills to manage a successful business. Our publications range from basic startup manuals to detailed guide books for implementing and managing a specific business.

A BUSINESS OF YOUR OWN does more than just present the nuts and bolts of initiating a business between the covers of a manual. We are different because entrepreneurial women are different! We also offer strategy sessions, workshops, seminars, business development retreats, and much more...

ABOUT OUR COMPREHENSIVE START UP MANUALS.......

The informational publications from *A BUSINESS OF YOUR OWN* reflect an enormous amount of in-depth research and the expertise of many noted professionals. Our comprehensive business start-up publications utilize a uniquely designed step-by-step, hands-on approach to business formulation. Crucial business development and management information is provided in an easy to understand format followed by questions for the entrepreneur to address. The summarization of the answers to these questions will enable the entrepreneurially minded woman in pulling together the major components of their business. Worksheets are provided for the purpose of providing assistance in preparing a business plan. All business start-up publications are designed so that upon completion, the entrepreneur will have a detailed business plan for their venture.

Our manuals are: *Currently researched *Informational *Practical *Systematic *Motivational *Comprehensive *Easy to understand *Designed for the Entrepreneurial Woman

Additional Publications for the Entrepreneurial Woman

- "So You're Thinking About Starting a Business" A Comprehensive General Start Up Manual" $49.95
- Starting a Secretarial Service $59.95
- Starting an Antique Business $59.95
- Starting a Public Relations Firm $59.95
- Starting a Flower Shop $59.95
- Starting a Clothing Boutique $59.95
- Starting a Business to Sell Your Craft Items $59.95
- Starting a Franchise $59.95
- Starting a Mail Order Business $59.95
- Starting a Gift Shop $59.95
- Starting a Home Based Business $59.95
- Starting a Business to Sell Your Art Work $59.95

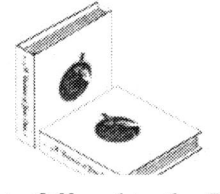

Shipping and Handling Costs: $4.00/manual ▲ *Traditional Discounts Offered to the Trade.*

A BUSINESS OF YOUR OWN
P.O.B. 210662 ■ Nashville, Tennessee 37221-0662
Phone: (615) 646-3708 ■ Fax: (615) 662-8584
E-mail: Success@womaninbiz.com   Website: www.womaninbiz.com

3 7219 00134 0119

J.S. Reynolds Community College

DISCARDED

```
HQ 778.5 .L68 2004
Lownes-Jackson, Millicent
 Gray.
Starting a child care center
```

J. SARGEANT REYNOLDS
COMMUNITY COLLEGE
Richmond, VA

Printed in the United States
18550LVS00001B/167-174

9 780943 267173